D0459129

OFFICIATING SOFTBALL

A publication for the National Federation of State High School
Associations Officials Education Program

Developed by the
American Sport Education Program

Human Kinetics

Library of Congress Cataloging-in-Publication Information

American Sport Education Program.
  Officiating Softball / American Sport Education Program with National Federation of State High School Associations.
      p. cm.
  Includes index.
  ISBN 0-7360-4764-6 (soft cover)
  1. Softball--Umpiring. I. National Federation of State High School Associations. II. Title.
  GV881.4.U47A54 2004
  796.357'8--dc22

                                    2004000579

ISBN: 0-7360-4764-6

The Web addresses cited in this text were current as of May 2004, unless otherwise noted.

NFHS Officials Education Program Coordinator and Project Consultant: Mary Struckhoff; **Project Writer:** Gareth Hancock; **Acquisitions Editors:** Renee Thomas Pyrtel and Greg George; **Developmental Editor:** Laura Pulliam; **Assistant Editors:** Scott Hawkins and Mandy Maiden; **Copyeditor:** Barbara Field; **Proofreader:** Sue Fetters; **Indexers:** Robert and Cynthia Swanson; **Graphic Designer:** Andrew Tietz; **Graphic Artist:** Francine Hamerski; **Photo Manager:** Dan Wendt; **Cover Designer:** Jack W. Davis; **Photographer (cover):** © National Federation of State High School Associations; **Photographer (interior):** Tom Roberts; photos on pages 1, 5, 10, 25, 127, 131, 137, 145, 149, 155, 157, 164, and 166 © Human Kinetics; **Art Manager:** Kareema McLendon; **Illustrators:** Keith Blomberg and Mic Greenberg; **Printer:** United Graphics

We thank Urbana High School in Urbana, Illinois, for assistance in providing the location for the photo shoot for this book.

Copies of this book are available at special discounts for bulk purchase for sales promotions, premiums, fundraising, or educational use. Special editions or book excerpts can also be created to specifications. For details, contact the Special Sales Manager at Human Kinetics.

Printed in the United States of America   10 9 8 7 6 5 4 3 2 1

Human Kinetics
Web site: www.HumanKinetics.com

United States: Human Kinetics
P.O. Box 5076
Champaign, IL 61825-5076
800-747-4457
e-mail: humank@hkusa.com

Canada: Human Kinetics
475 Devonshire Road Unit 100
Windsor, ON N8Y 2L5
800-465-7301 (in Canada only)
e-mail: orders@hkcanada.com

Europe: Human Kinetics
107 Bradford Road
Stanningley
Leeds LS28 6AT, United Kingdom
+44 (0) 113 255 5665
e-mail: hk@hkeurope.com

Australia: Human Kinetics
57A Price Avenue
Lower Mitcham, South Australia 5062
08 8277 1555
e-mail: liaw@hkaustralia.com

New Zealand: Human Kinetics
Division of Sports Distributors NZ Ltd.
P.O. Box 300 226 Albany
North Shore City
Auckland
0064 9 448 1207
e-mail: blairc@hknewz.com

CONTENTS

PREFACE

Umpires are an essential part of both slow-pitch and fast-pitch softball, but how do softball umpires come to know their stuff? How do they keep every rule and mechanic straight throughout each game and through every season? Educational tools and reference materials such as this manual will help every official not only learn their craft, but also stay sharp. *Officiating Softball* is a key resource for you if you want to umpire softball games at the high school level. The mechanics you'll find here were developed by the National Federation of State High School Associations (NFHS) and are used for high school softball throughout the United States.

We expect you know at least a little about softball, but maybe not much about officiating it. On the other end of the spectrum, you might know lots about both. But the overall objective of *Officiating Softball* is to prepare you to officiate games, no matter what your level of experience. More specifically, this book will

- introduce you to the culture of officiating softball,
- tell you what will be expected of you as a softball umpire,
- explain and illustrate in detail the mechanics of officiating softball,
- show a connection between the rules of softball and the mechanics of officiating it and
- serve as a reference throughout your officiating career.

Officiating Softball covers softball officiating basics, mechanics and specific play situations. In part I, you'll read about who softball umpires are and what qualities you'll find in a good umpire. Part I also differentiates high school officiating from officiating at youth and college levels and describes game responsibilities, including pregame and postgame duties. Part II, the meat of the book, describes plate and base umpire mechanics and one-, two- and three-umpire systems, all in careful detail. You'll find these chapters well organized and amply illustrated. Part III highlights some key cases from the *NFHS Softball Case Book* and shows how you, the umpire, can apply the rules in action.

Officiating Softball is a practical how-to resource that's approved by the NFHS. This book can also be used with the *NFHS Officiating Softball Methods* online course, which was also developed and produced by the American Sport Education Program (ASEP) as part of the NFHS Officials Education Program. To find out how to register for the online course, visit www.ASEP.com.

NFHS OFFICIALS CODE OF ETHICS

Officials at an interscholastic athletic event are participants in the educational development of high school students. As such, they must exercise a high level of self-discipline, independence and responsibility. The purpose of this code is to establish guidelines for ethical standards of conduct for all interscholastic officials.

- Officials shall master both the rules of the game and the mechanics necessary to enforce the rules and shall exercise authority in an impartial, firm and controlled manner.
- Officials shall work with each other and their state associations in a constructive and cooperative manner.
- Officials shall uphold the honor and dignity of the profession in all interactions with student-athletes, coaches, athletic directors, school administrators, colleagues and the public.
- Officials shall prepare themselves both physically and mentally, shall dress neatly and appropriately, and shall comport themselves in a manner consistent with the high standards of the profession.
- Officials shall be punctual and professional in the fulfillment of all contractual obligations.
- Officials shall remain mindful that their conduct influences the respect that student-athletes, coaches and the public hold for the profession.
- Officials shall, while enforcing the rules of play, remain aware of the inherent risk of injury that competition poses to student-athletes. Where appropriate, they shall inform event management of conditions or situations that appear unreasonably hazardous.
- Officials shall take reasonable steps to educate themselves in the recognition of emergency conditions that might arise during competition.

KEY TO DIAGRAMS

 Umpire starting position

 Umpire ending position

 Player

• • •   Batted ball

- - -   Umpire path

PART I

SOFTBALL OFFICIATING
BASICS

CHAPTER 1

INTRODUCTION TO SOFTBALL OFFICIATING

Softball has a long history as one of the most popular high school sports in North America, with thousands of competitive teams hitting the fields every spring. Key to the success of the sport are the umpires, like you, who ensure safe and fair competition through a firm grasp of the rules, a solid understanding of umpiring mechanics and the use of sound judgment in managing game situations.

Softball umpires come from all walks of life, with many having been athletes in younger years, but common among them is a love of competition and a desire to stay involved with the game. You may have played softball or baseball at some level, or perhaps you were drawn to the game through friends, family or others in your community. Whether female or male, experienced or just learning, you are performing a valuable service that allows today's youth to excel and to learn and challenge themselves. Learn your craft well and be proud of your service. You are part of a community of professionals dedicated to upholding high standards of fair play that allows student-athletes to experience the excitement and personal growth that comes from competing in team sports.

If you are just beginning to learn officiating, there is much you can do to prepare yourself before heading to the field for the first time. For all readers, including those who have called games before, this manual will serve as a complete reference of officiating mechanics that you will want to keep close at hand.

In addition to studying this manual, you can improve your umpiring by actively engaging with the growing community of softball umpires. Whether you are comparing notes with other umpires after a game or exchanging thoughts with professionals from around the country, your colleagues offer a wealth of knowledge and experience to draw from. Before you know it, you will be stepping onto the field with the confidence of a veteran!

Purpose and Philosophy

As an umpire, your job is to manage the game by enforcing rules effectively such that participants experience the excitement of the sport in an atmosphere of fair and safe competition. Good officiating is founded on the following three keys:

1. You must have complete knowledge of the rules to ensure fair play.
2. You must use sound judgment in exercising your authority to control the game.
3. You need to use proper officiating mechanics to be in the right place at the right time.

Knowing the Rules

To be a competent umpire, you need to have a firm grasp of all the rules of softball. New and experienced umpires alike should devote ample time to reading and studying the *NFHS Softball Rules Book*. As an umpire, you are expected to have a complete grasp of the entire body of rules and regulations—you cannot do your job effectively without this knowledge. Rather than trying to learn the mechanics in this book or the entire *NFHS Softball Rules Book* in a single sitting, you will be more likely to retain the information if you study 30 to 60 minutes a day over a few weeks. As with any new skill, umpiring takes time and patience to learn.

Each year, rules are revised. Umpires must stay current by constantly reviewing and studying the rules. It may sound obvious, but you cannot apply the rules if you do not know them. Keep in mind, however, that even the most experienced umpires refer to the *NFHS Softball Rules Book*, so don't expect to memorize every rule immediately if you are a new umpire. The more you umpire games, the more the rules and mechanics will become second nature to you. Discussing the rules with fellow umpires before, after and outside of games is another great way to master the rules and regulations of softball.

Using Sound Judgment

Even more important than understanding the rules of the game is your use of sound judgment in applying them. Because softball is a complex game with many possible scenarios, the rules are quite extensive. But even with the large number of rules, not every situation or nuance can be anticipated and accounted for precisely in the *NFHS Softball Rules Book*. As the game's governing authority, it is up to you to handle all game situations by interpreting and applying rules in a way that minimizes player risk and provides for fair competition.

Examples of the need for judgment might be a location-specific occurrence, such as whether the field is playable after a lengthy rain delay, or perhaps an angry fan or coach inappropriately disrupting the game. Get clear in your mind your primary mission—to minimize risk and ensure a fair game for all—and make any decisions not explicitly accounted for by the rules with this single goal firmly in mind. Through experience and likely some hard knocks, you will gain the poise and thick skin that enables a good umpire to manage ambiguous situations fairly or take even the most disagreeable incidents in stride. It helps to be mentally and emotionally prepared, but by exercising control and sound judgment, you will manage such situations effectively and keep the game on track.

Umpires must use sound judgment to ensure that the game is played fairly and safely.

Using Proper Officiating Mechanics

Softball is an action-packed, dynamic sport that requires you to hustle, to be in the right place at the right time, to make calls effectively and to stay out of the way of the players. In addition to the rules of the game, there are detailed guidelines for different umpiring systems that specify where you should be on the field for any given game situation. Different umpire positions are used depending on the number of umpires officiating a game. Each system (one, two and three umpires) is explained in detail in part II of this book.

Just as with the rules, you must know the field mechanics of each system for each of the umpire positions on the field. You may be called on to be the plate umpire or any of the base umpires, and each role has a different set of responsibilities. The performance of these responsibilities is critical to umpiring a game effectively. You will make great strides toward being respected as a competent softball umpire if you know where you need to be for every play and hustle to get there. After some study and experience, these positioning requirements will not only make sense, they will become instinctive for you.

Essential Equipment for Every Umpire

You need several pieces of equipment to perform your duties as an umpire. These include your uniform, safety equipment if you are umpiring the plate and other tools you will use throughout the game.

Uniform

- *Shoes.* Solid black, comfortable, well shined
- *Socks.* Black
- *Pants and shirt.* Heather gray pants, powder blue shirt, wrinkle-free
- *Belt.* Black
- *Umpire's cap.* Navy blue, sized, in good shape, worn forward
- *Jacket.* Navy blue

Plate Umpire Safety Equipment

- Leg guards
- Inside-style chest protector
- Face mask with throat protector
- Protective cup (male umpires)
- Hard or steel-reinforced shoes

Accessories

- *Brush.* For both plate and base umpires to clean home plate, the pitcher's plate and bases.
- *Bat ring.* To check bats to ensure compliance with size regulations.
- *Ball bag (plate umpire).* For extra game balls, lineups and pencil.
- *Indicator.* For counting balls, strikes and outs.
- *Coin.* For deciding the home team, if necessary.
- *Paper and pencil.* For recording warnings, charged conferences and substitutions (on lineup cards).
- *Water.* To help you stay fresh, especially on hot days; water jugs should be placed outside the field.
- *NFHS Softball Rules Book.* You never know when you might need to clarify an obscure rule; have one nearby, but do not take it on the field.

Before you leave home for the game, be sure you have your uniform and all necessary tools with you. There is nothing worse than showing up without a key piece of equipment. Even if you are planning to umpire the bases, bring all your equipment with you, just in case!

There are three main reasons for learning and following the mechanics guidelines. First, by doing so, you will be in a good position at the right time to make a call. Second, by knowing where you need to go, you can concentrate more fully on the call itself. And third, by knowing and doing your job, you allow your partners to focus on their own responsibilities. Using good mechanics simplifies the job of making calls, so be sure to learn and follow the field movement guidelines.

Field mechanics tell you where you should be, and hustling is how you should get there. On your list of relatively simple things you can do to become a good softball umpire is moving quickly and decisively to the right position for a call, keeping in mind that your viewing angle is even more important than your distance from the play. You are not hustling for the sake of it; you are doing it to be in the best possible position to make a good call. Thus, being in good enough physical shape to hustle throughout an entire game is very important.

What Makes a Good Softball Official?

In addition to the three keys introduced above, the following 10 points will go a long way toward helping you become a capable and respected softball umpire:

1. Stay in shape and look the part.

You should stay physically fit throughout the entire softball season so fatigue is never a factor in your ability to officiate a game. Softball games often last as long as two to three hours, which means you will be placing great demands on your body. You need to be mentally alert for the entire game, and you will have greater difficulty keeping track of game situations if you are straining to get into position or are huffing and puffing when you arrive to call a play! Today's athletes are in great shape, making for a very fast-paced game. An umpire who is not physically fit enough to follow proper field mechanics in a timely manner will likely be a detriment to the game.

Related to physical conditioning is the importance of a professional appearance. Dressing the part will not only help you command greater respect from players and fans; it will make it easier to perform your job.

2. Make decisions firmly and promptly.

Calls must be made definitively and promptly, but you should not be too hasty in calling a play. You must guard against making or announcing decisions prematurely because you cannot make a good call until the play has been completed. You need to move quickly to get into position for a play, yet come to a stop before the culmination point, so you can see all the action clearly before making a ruling. Just as it is much harder for a player to catch a ball while running, it is more difficult for an umpire to make the correct call while in motion. Anticipate plays, and try to be in position, stopped and physically balanced when viewing a play.

After a momentary hesitation to make certain the play is complete, you should make the call clearly and forcefully. An uncertain or timid call will be perceived as a lack of confidence, which is an invitation for objection and argument. Calling plays with an air of confidence goes a long way toward having your judgment accepted. A strong, definitive voice is a valuable asset.

3. Work as a team.

Crew cohesiveness is important for effectively umpiring a game and also for showing that all umpires are "on the same page." Cohesiveness is obtained through positive, effective communication and mutual support and respect. On the field, you all share the same goal—doing a great job controlling the game—and you should work together with that firmly in mind. An ideal rapport with your fellow umpires is friendly, professional and supportive. Focus on your specific responsibilities and have confidence that other umpires will manage their responsibilities. All umpires should strive to support other officiating partners throughout the entire contest. When one umpire requests an opinion from another concerning a call, the opinion should be given honestly and courteously only to the umpire requesting it. Never offer an unsolicited opinion. Providing unsolicited advice to other umpires is inappropriate and disruptive and will lead to a lack of confidence in the officials among players and coaches.

Do not discuss decisions with anyone but your officiating partners, and then do so only in private when requested or requesting to do so. Partners should always be honest with each other when discussing plays. Without neglecting your responsibilities, be aware of all game play as much as possible to be in a position to help if requested by another umpire. Call in your own area, but observe in all areas. That said, there may be situations where you simply do not see a play outside your scope of responsibility, in which case an honest admission that you did not see the play is acceptable.

4. Know the rules.

As mentioned previously, good umpiring is largely dependent on a complete knowledge and understanding of the rules. Some decisions are common enough that, with experience, they become instinctive. A great way to practice your decision making is through constant study of possible game situations. When watching games in person or on television, consider how you would apply rules in the situations that arise. If you do not know how to handle a situation, write it down and research it to get the answer. If you have a question about a particular game situation, officiating peers, local and state officials associations and the NFHS online officials forum are great places to get opinions and interpretations.

Analyzing game "case studies" is an excellent way to increase your familiarity with the rules and improve your reaction time. Reading the *NFHS Softball Rules Book* thoroughly many times is important, but you will be far better able to apply the rules when you are in a game if you approach them through scenarios instead of just memorization. Part III of this book, "Applying the Rules," provides several case studies, organized by game area, to help you begin to think like an umpire. In addition to this, veteran and new umpires alike should attend rules clinics whenever possible to keep abreast of rule changes and recommended interpretations.

5. Know the field mechanics.

Proper umpiring mechanics are essential to play coverage. The most knowledgeable umpire will be much less effective if he or she fails to be in the prescribed position to make a call. Mechanics, or play coverage, must be mastered for you to be successful. As with knowing the rules, consider your placement and movement as you watch other softball games. Officiating clinics provide a good opportunity to review positioning and coverage as well as a chance to practice outside of game situations. You need to be able to get into the best possible position for any given play without being in the way of any player or a thrown or batted ball.

6. Ignore spectators.

Your job is to umpire and manage the game, not to discuss or negotiate game outcomes with fans. Spectators, contrary to what *they* might think, are not part of the game's action. Difficult as it may be, you must do your job as if they did not exist. This means ignoring remarks, including heckling and criticism and a wide range of body language and other actions. However, recognize that certain language and behaviors are unacceptable at any school activity and need to be handled appropriately. If overly offensive or disruptive fan behavior occurs, you should notify the field administrator to handle the situation. If no field administrator is present, enlist the help of the home team coach.

7. Make the call without showboating.

Softball is about the players' opportunity to shine, not yours. Although umpires' techniques and on-field personalities will vary, your vocal and physical expression of calls and rulings should be consistent and controlled, not overly showy or distracting. Discharging your responsibility with dignity and in conformance with accepted signals and procedures will encourage the players and spectators to accept the decisions you make. This does not mean you cannot exhibit some flair of your own, but it should never be distracting or overly dramatic. In short, umpires should be part of the game, but never the center of attention.

8. Keep the game moving.

Players should hustle on and off the field between innings, and many will take their cues from your behavior. If you hustle, they are more likely to do so also. Similarly, try to manage delays such as a batter being late to the plate or unnecessarily long warm-ups between innings. Enforcing the one-minute or five-pitches-between-innings rules will significantly speed up the game. Your goal is not to rush the pace, but not to let games drag either.

9. Be courteous but not overly friendly.

Be courteous and responsive to players and coaches, but avoid visiting with them during or immediately before or after the game. By working to create a businesslike attitude and atmosphere, you will be better able to control the game. Do not get into arguments with the players, coaches or team representatives. Any discussion should be brief and to the point. A dignified and confident attitude will often prevent an argument. Be polite and professional at all times.

10. Recognize that everyone makes mistakes.

Even the best umpires make mistakes, and you will too. When this happens, you need to keep your cool, shake it off and move on. Do not be embarrassed or show any emotion regarding the call. And keep firmly in mind that each call must be made entirely based on the facts of the specific situation. As much as you might feel the urge to "even things up," do not give in to it. A second bad call will not make up for the first one—it will only make things worse. Know your job, hustle and make the calls to the best of your ability.

Umpires should encourage players to hustle between innings to keep the game moving.

Softball Umpire's Tools

There are several tools you can use to learn and practice officiating:

- *The current rules book*. Get it, study it, study it again, then study it *again*. Knowing the rules cold will be your best ally when you are on the field and on the spot. NFHS rules are modified annually, so make sure you are working from the latest version of the rules.
- *Educational resources*. Use this book and the *Officiating Softball Mechanics CD (NFHS Edition)* that shows animated mechanics to really drive home key points visually. Also, plug in to the community—magazines and Web sites can be a great way to pick up tricks of the trade.
- *Watch and learn*. Watch other umpires in action, in person or on television. As you watch, consider where you would position yourself, how you would make the call, and also, study the way they use their authority to control the game.
- *Talk to colleagues*. You have joined a group of dedicated professionals, and part of your responsibility is to help one another, so do not be shy. If you do not understand something, ask someone who knows to explain it to you. When you become a master of softball officiating, return the favor.
- *Clinics and workshops*. This book will give you an excellent grounding, but do not let your education stop here. Most areas have clinics you can attend (the NFHS Web site is a great place to locate regional associations and information), and it will be worth your while to do so. You will learn, meet new colleagues and probably even have fun while becoming a better umpire.
- *First-hand experience*. Last but certainly not least, get on the field as often as you can and use every game to improve your skills. Is there a casual softball league in your area? You can get great practice by volunteering to umpire more casual softball games.

Officiating at the High School Level

Umpiring softball at the high school level is similar in most respects to umpiring softball at lower and higher levels such as youth, college or professional. If you have officiated at other levels and are making the transition to high school softball, you'll need to learn about a few differences, but most of the rules and mechanics are the same.

The main difference between youth and high school softball is the stricter definition of your role as umpire. Where an umpire in youth softball sometimes plays the role of coach to help less-experienced players understand the game and do their best, such stretching of roles does not occur in high school softball. The coaches have their job and you have yours, and the two do not overlap. Your job is to call the game fairly and professionally.

If you have umpired at higher levels, the mechanics of high school officiating are much the same. However, you need to be aware of several rule differences. Similarly, high school leagues or divisions may use different umpiring systems ranging from having a single umpire call all aspects of the game to two-, three- and even four-umpire systems where each base is covered by a different umpire.

It is somewhat unusual (and challenging) to call a game as a single umpire, but this system is occasionally employed, typically only for slow-pitch softball. The two-umpire system is common during regular season play and offers solid field coverage and good distribution of responsibilities. Three- and four-umpire systems are sometimes used during end-of-season playoffs or tournaments and are less common during regular season play. Chapter 5 describes in detail how the mechanics work in each of the different systems. As you are learning to officiate, you should gain familiarity with each of these different umpiring systems, as you never know when or where your officiating services might be needed! You should, however, devote most study to the system used predominantly by your high school association.

As a softball umpire, you can become a member of the NFHS Officials Association, which provides support and professional opportunities for high school officials. It is the only officials association in the United States for high school sports officials, with a membership of more than 130,000 people across all 50 states.

The NFHS Officials Association's parent organization, the National Federation of State High School Associations, exists to serve its members and related professional groups by leading and coordinating the administration of interscholastic activities to enhance the educational experiences of high school students. The NFHS works to promote participation in scholastic activities, sporting behavior and equitable opportunities among high school students with the greater goal of creating good citizens.

Becoming a great softball umpire takes dedication and experience, and this chapter has described many steps you can take to get yourself well on the way to earning the respect and appreciation of student athletes, coaches and your entire community. The remainder of this book explains the fundamentals of good officiating, from basic field mechanics to on-field conflict management and everything in between. However, the learning should not stop here. You have joined a dynamic and supportive community of professionals who will help you learn and gain confidence as an umpire.

CHAPTER 2

GAME PROCEDURES AND RESPONSIBILITIES

To ensure adequate field coverage, officiating teams consist of a plate umpire and either one, two or three base umpires. Each umpire has a clearly identified set of coverage responsibilities depending on the number of officials working a game. In addition to controlling game play, each umpire must perform several pre- and postgame tasks to start and complete a softball game effectively.

Plate and Base Umpire Responsibilities

The plate umpire is responsible for calling the action at home plate, including balls and strikes, many fly and foul balls and nearly all plays that occur at the plate, as well as for recording conferences and substitutions. Base officials have designated areas of responsibility in the infield and outfield and also play a supporting role in helping the plate umpire control the game. To make the game go smoothly, all officials must work together as a team from the moment they arrive at the game site to the time they depart. Plate and base umpire mechanics are discussed in detail in part II, but the following describes the basic set of responsibilities.

The plate umpire has additional responsibilities before, throughout and after the game. These responsibilities include the following:

- Leading the pregame conference, including making introductions among officials, coaches and team captains.
- Determining forfeits, if necessary. You should do everything possible (that is also fair and safe) to avoid a forfeit.
- Obtaining and tracking the official lineups on lineup cards for both teams, including substitution management throughout the game. The plate umpire is responsible for recording team warnings on the back of cards.

- Maintaining control of game balls during and between innings and returning them to the site manager at the end of the game.
- Reporting any flagrantly improper conduct to site or association authorities after the game.

Base umpires must participate in pregame and other essential conferences to be informed about any special field considerations (such as an unusual field feature or any local rules). Similarly, base umpires need to be aware of everything that occurs during a game to contribute to the overall game-control effort. The plate umpire has additional umpiring responsibilities as the leader of the umpiring crew, but he or she needs the support and contributions of all umpires to manage the game in the best manner possible.

Base umpires have specific coverage responsibilities, which are detailed in chapters 4 and 5. As with any team activity, communication is key to success.

Other responsibilities unique to base umpires include monitoring certain catch/no-catch and fair/foul situations in the outfield, watching to be sure runners touch bases and calling plays at any bases for which they are responsible. As a base umpire, you may also be called on by the plate umpire to rule on a possible checked swing (thus, you should be positioned correctly and watching the batter attentively on every pitch). You also need to watch for illegal pitches, watch runners closely in tag-up situations, keep the pitcher's plate clean, make sure bases are securely fastened and more! There is a lot to keep track of, but with time and practice, these responsibilities will become second nature for you.

Pregame Procedures and Responsibilities

Several items must be taken care of before the plate umpire can call, "Play ball!" and get the game officially under way. These responsibilities start even before the actual game day, as you should confirm the date, time and location of the game you are scheduled for in advance with the school and your umpiring partners (imagine the sinking feeling you would have showing up to an empty ball field!). Also, if you are still learning the officiating ropes, take the time to review the rules and mechanics the day before a game so they are fresh in your mind on game day. Last, make certain you are well groomed and your uniform is clean and neat so that you look professional when you step on the field.

Pregame procedures involve meeting with your umpiring crew, performing equipment and field safety checks, clarifying rules and mechanics, addressing field irregularities or ground rules (Is that area near the bleachers in or out of play? What about that pool of standing water in right field?), obtaining official team lineups and resolving other questions that may come into play during the game. These standard pregame procedures ensure that officials, coaches and athletes are all "on the same page" before the game begins, thereby eliminating ambiguities and reducing the chance for misunderstandings or surprises.

Plate and base umpires have different pregame responsibilities. If you are a less experienced umpire, be sure to use this pregame period to address any questions or concerns you have with other members of your officiating crew. Remember that it is far better to admit to your fellow crew members that you do not know something before a game than to demonstrate to everyone that you do not know something during a game! If you are unsure about anything, ask for clarification. As a side note, if necessary, you can use the time between innings to ask questions of more experienced umpires; however, be sure to keep such conversations private to avoid losing the confidence of the players and coaches.

Both plate and base umpires must arrive at the playing field at least 30 minutes before the scheduled time of the game to allow time to prepare for and perform all pregame duties. Arriving late and having to rush through pregame responsibilities will set a hurried and disorganized pace that will be hard to recover from throughout the game. Making a good first impression with everyone involved is very important. Arriving in time to complete your pregame duties in a professional manner will generate immediate respect among players, coaches and fans and will make your job as umpire much easier.

Once all umpires arrive at the game site, let the coaches and game administrators know you are there. Confirm the current time and starting time for the game so that everyone is on the same schedule. Check that the host administration has provided a game ball to each team for warm-up. Be friendly but professional, completing your tasks purposefully.

Ground Rules

The umpire crew should tour the field together prior to game time to identify any special field situations that may come into play during the game. All obstacles that could create dead-ball situations should be carefully noted and considered. Ground rules must be established prior to the start of the game. Ground rules define the playing area and are separate from official NFHS game rules (see "What Are Ground Rules?" on page 16). Review ground rules with the home team or facilities representative prior to the formal pregame conference to ensure that all umpires have a firm understanding of any location-specific rules. The plate umpire must confer with the coaches on any nonstandard ground rules and review them at the coach and player pregame conference. Keep in mind that

Softball parks vary greatly in design, construction and condition. Part of your job as an umpire is to make sure that, before the game starts, everyone has the same understanding of any special rules required due to field irregularities. These special field-dependent rules are referred to as ground rules. The ground-rule decisions made should minimize player risk as much as possible. You should carefully evaluate all possible scenarios where a field irregularity could affect game play ahead of time to avoid disruptions by an unanticipated situation. Lay down the law early to avoid having to form additional rules during the game.

Make sure the field is properly marked and all field equipment complies with official field regulations (see figure 2.1 for the basic layout of a regulation field). For example, the pitcher's plate and bases must be legal equipment and must be positioned at the proper locations and distances; foul poles at the end of the foul lines extending past first and third base should be painted a distinct color or have flags attached to identify them; and any walls that limit the outfield near the foul line should have vertical foul-line markings on them. Following is a list of a few common ground rules that are often adopted in cases

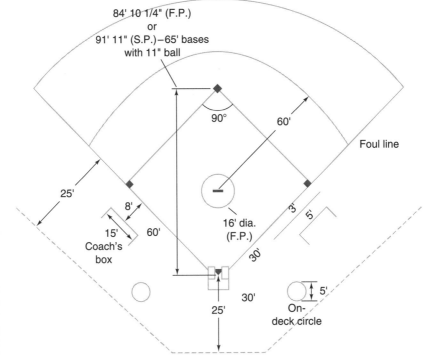

FIGURE 2.1   Regulation softball field.

where the field does not meet the specifications provided in the *NFHS Softball Rules Book*:

1. *Field obstructions.* If a batted ball goes behind an obstruction, such as fan bleachers or a fence, it is ruled a dead ball. It is recommended that no obstruction be less than 25 feet from the diamond, but not all fields are designed this way.

2. *Live ball out of play.* Wild pitches, overthrows and fair batted balls that go over or through a fence or into a dugout (out of play) can entitle runners to awarded bases. If the field has unusual obstructions, ground rules should, as nearly as possible, be similar to this rule.

3. *Dead ball due to field conditions.* For special field conditions that make fielding a ball slow or difficult (for example, a drain pipe cover that hides or impedes access to a ball, making retrieval difficult), the ball should become dead and each runner's advance should be limited to one or two bases. Be sure to identify any such dead-ball field spots prior to the start of the game, and inform fielders what they should do if a ball goes into such an area. The fielder should stand up with hands raised to let umpires know to verify that the ball is out of play. Once this is done, the runners should be placed at their proper bases.

4. *Unfenced fields.* On unfenced fields, a chalk line or imaginary out-of-play line should be established prior to the game to define the live-ball area (if the ball is in this area, runners may advance an unlimited number of bases with the risk of being put out by the defensive team). One common scenario is to have a parking lot with cars parked along the out-of-play line. This is both a player risk and game-play issue. Umpires should consider this parking area as if it were bleacher seats and call the ball dead if it enters the area.

The main point to keep in mind is that you need to clarify any such ground rules with players and coaches before starting the game.

ground rules may not supersede a rule in the *NFHS Softball Rules Book*. For example, the NFHS rules do not allow for a "ground-rule triple," which is a three-base award for a batted ball that goes into dead-ball territory. If coaches cannot reach agreement on a ground rule, the plate umpire should make the final decision. Try to adopt ground rules that keep the ball in play as much as possible, as opposed to creating additional dead-ball situations. In ballparks that are not completely fenced in, the umpire should establish an out-of-play area down the left- and right-field lines, usually paralleling the foul lines and starting at the backstop, continuing through the team bench/dugout area and out away from home plate. Try to line up a permanent object (such as a tree or building) visually from home plate through the dugout bench to make it easier to determine whether a ball is in or out of play.

Equipment Check

As part of the pregame safety and rule compliance check, you must evaluate both teams' equipment to verify that it meets official safety requirements. Playing sports has inherent risk, but national, state and local associations work hard to minimize that risk through specific and carefully determined equipment standards. The *NFHS Softball Rules Book* includes discussion about acceptable equipment that you should become familiar with. Be sure to do your part to verify that all equipment checks out before the game gets under way. You are the on-site agent responsible for making sure that carefully crafted rules and regulations are enforced. If a helmet, bat or other piece of equipment is not sanctioned under the current rules, it is up to you to ensure it never becomes part of the game.

This equipment check is standard procedure and should not be interpreted by coaches or players as suspicion of unfair play. Nevertheless, as a courtesy, you should inform each team's coach prior to inspecting the equipment. You need to check softballs, bats, batting helmets, catcher's equipment and any other equipment present for compliance with NFHS rules and regulations. The burden of proof for the legality of equipment is usually or typically on the teams and coaches. Last, make sure that all equipment is kept behind the out-of-play line to avoid accidents during the game. Similarly, players who are not required to be on the field for game play should remain in the dugout or bench area throughout the game.

Umpires' Pregame Conference

The umpiring crew (assuming there is more than one umpire) should meet before the start of the game to privately review ground rules, general rules, if necessary, and the distribution of umpiring responsibilities. More specifically, you should do the following:

- *Discuss any new rules.* Has anything changed recently? Make sure you have a current *NFHS Softball Rules Book*, *NFHS Softball Case Book* and this manual available for reference. All umpires are expected to have a firm grasp of softball rules, so basic rules are generally not discussed at the umpires' conference unless there is a special reason to do so. However, as a newer official, if you do not know something, ask your colleagues!

- *Review field ground rules.* You should already have toured the field, and the plate umpire should already have spoken with the field administrator or home field representative to get the "scoop" on any field irregularities. Discussion in the umpires' conference is intended to ensure that all umpires are well informed and in agreement.
- *Discuss foul-line and dead-ball area coverage.* Who will handle what in terms of foul balls? Under what situations?
- *Discuss base coverage.* Talk about coverage in terms of calling plays such as out/safe and tag/no tag. Make sure everyone is clear on how base rotation will occur (see chapter 5 for more on this subject). Also, review base coverage, including players not touching a base or leaving a base too soon, and how an appeal will be handled.
- *Review pitching rules.* Clarify what constitutes an illegal pitch and who is responsible for calling different aspects of it.
- *Discuss checked swing mechanics.* Who is responsible for the call? How should checked swing requests be handled?
- *Review communication expectations between umpires.* A useful umpire's saying is, "If we deviate, communicate!"
- *Review the pregame procedures.* What are the pregame conference procedures? Do coaches and captains attend? What needs to be covered? Who will say what? Are there any special issues to cover?
- *Consider any special pregame announcements or ceremonies.* These may include the national anthem, introduction of players or any awards ceremonies.
- *Check equipment.* If you are the plate umpire, make sure you have a pen, brush (to keep the plate clean), count indicator, mask and ball bag.
- *Discuss signals.* Talk through any verbal or visual signals to be used among the umpires to assist with calls.

At the end of the umpires' conference, you should be clear on all rules and be ready to hold the coach and player pregame conference. See "Pregame Checklist" on page 20 for a reproducible list of an umpire's duties prior to the start of a game.

Coach and Player Pregame Conference

The formal coach and player pregame conference is the final important step before game play can begin. As an umpire, this is your chance to set the tone for the entire game with both teams. What you cover and how you cover it is critical to game play and your success as an umpire. Most coaches, unless they are very new, will be familiar with this part of the pregame proceedings. Conduct the conference with a positive,

_____ 1. Notify the management or the home team coach immediately upon your arrival.

_____ 2. Gather with your crewmates for a pregame conference to prepare for the game. This includes discussing positioning, how to deal with timing plays, how to handle assistance needed on checked swings and foul balls, and ground rules.

_____ 3. Closely examine the playing field, making certain that it is properly marked, that the pitcher's plate is legal in every respect and that you are familiar with the boundaries, fences and screens. As you examine the field, note all obstacles that could create dead-ball situations. Look for potential safety problems or risks. It is best for the crew to tour the field together so that any points or questions concerning safety and ground rules can be considered and the conclusion made known to the appropriate individuals.

_____ 4. Ten minutes before the scheduled game time, move onto the field. Check each team's equipment to make sure it is legal and safe. The plate umpire should check the visitors; a base umpire should check the home team. Bats, helmets and catcher masks/helmet combinations must be thoroughly inspected. Batting helmets and catcher's helmets must have the National Operating Coommittee on Standards for Athletic Equipment (NOCSAE) seal. Any illegal or unsafe equipment must be brought to the attention of the coach and should be stored so that they will not be used during the game.

_____ 5. At least five minutes prior to the scheduled starting time, the umpires and team coaches and/or team captains should meet at home plate for a pregame conference to check lineups (home team first) and to discuss ground rules and any other pertinent matters. Ask coaches whether all their players are legally and properly equipped, and share your expectation that they exhibit good sporting behavior. Don't forget to check about the Designated Player (DP/FLEX) rule. If the game involves tournament play, it may be necessary to toss a coin to determine which team is the home team if this has not been previously determined by the tournament manager.

_____ 6. Make sure the official scorer has been provided with copies of the two starting batting orders after you have inspected the cards to eliminate any errors in recording. Check the data with the scorer and correct any errors in transmission.

_____ 7. Briefly discuss with the official scorer such matters as the proper batting orders and the appearance of pinch hitters and substitutes. This matter is particularly important in interscholastic games because of the re-entry and DP/FLEX rule.

From *Officiating Softball* by ASEP, 2004, Champaign, IL: Human Kinetics.

confident demeanor and a firm voice to make certain you are understood and also to establish your authority. Following are the steps to take for a pregame conference:

1. *Positioning.* The plate umpire will do most of the talking and should be positioned behind home plate facing the outfield, with each team's coaches and captains on either side of home plate. The base umpire(s) should stand opposite the plate umpire, facing the backstop.

2. *Introductions.* The plate umpire should handle introductions among the umpiring crew, coaches and captains in attendance.

3. *Review the ground rules.* Begin by outlining dead-ball areas at home plate, and then carry the discussion clockwise around the perimeter of the playing area—along the third-base dugout/bench area, outfield fence and foul poles, and finally the first-base dugout/bench area. Reviewing the field in this circumferential manner will ensure that you do not accidentally miss any areas. Cover all openings, obstacles or special situations to ensure that you can identify and answer any questions raised. If an issue arises that has not been previously decided, ask the coach of the home team if there is a standard procedure for the field. If so, and both sides agree to it, endorse it as official. If there is no standard for the irregularity, make a recommendation and attempt to reach consensus between the teams. Be reasonable in accepting other opinions or suggestions, but keep in mind that as plate umpire, you have final authority to make a ruling. Also keep in mind that no ground rule can supersede any NFHS official rule. Be sure the difference between live-ball and dead-ball territory is understood by all.

4. *Review the lineup cards.* Explain the importance of notifying the plate umpire of substitutes. Make sure first and last names are listed for all players, starters and substitutes and that each player's defensive position and uniform number are listed. A good practice is to hand the lineup cards back to each coach after they have been submitted to you and ask them to check the lineups one last time before making them official. This is an optional courtesy, but it is a good one. Mistakes happen, and it is far better to identify and fix them before the game starts than to receive special lineup requests (which are not allowed) from an embarrassed and anguished coach! A copy of the final and official lineup card should be provided to the official scorer prior to the start of the game. The plate umpire should briefly discuss key scoring matters with the official scorer, such as how pinch hitters, courtesy runners and substitutes will be handled. This matter is particularly important in both fast- and slow-pitch softball because of the player reentry rule, which can

make substitutions more complicated. Specifically, it is important for fast-pitch games because of the DP/FLEX rule and for slow-pitch games because of the Extra Player (EP) rule.

Also, for fast-pitch softball, if there is a DP/FLEX, you must make sure there are 10 players in each starting lineup. If there is no DP/FLEX, there should only be 9 players on each card. For slow pitch, make sure 10 players are listed, or 11 if using the optional EP rule. *Note:* To use the optional EP or DP/FLEX, a team must submit it on the lineup prior to the game.

5. *Discuss time between games, if applicable.* If umpiring a doubleheader, discuss how much time will be allotted between the two games.

6. *Remind teams of the official score book.* This book is managed by the home team, and both team's scorekeepers should verify the statistics with each other several times throughout the game. As an umpire, if you identify an obvious scoring error during the game, you have the authority to correct it.

7. *Remind teams of the procedure for asking questions.* If a question arises during the game, only the team's coach should approach the umpire responsible for the call and should do so in a sporting manner.

8. *Wrap up the meeting.* Ask if there are any questions. If so, answer them in a friendly, professional tone. Finally, review NFHS expectations regarding sporting behavior, wish the coaches and players a good game and conclude the meeting.

As you can see, there is a lot to take care of before the game even starts. Arriving at the game site early is important for many reasons. Your pregame work lays the foundation on which you will umpire the game, and you want it to be a strong and positive start. After carefully completing the pregame obligations, it's time for the plate umpire to set the game in motion with a hearty, "Play ball!" Did you know that starting the game with this traditional call is actually an official rule in the *NFHS Softball Rules Book*?

Chapters 3 through 5 cover the details and mechanics of umpiring game action, but first we will complete the "bookends" of the game by discussing postgame procedures.

Postgame Procedures and Responsibilities

Once the last out has been called or the winning run has been scored and the game is officially over, you have completed all the hard work—congratulations! But there are still a few postgame tasks to complete, as well

Ball Rotation Procedure

According to NFHS procedure, the current game ball should remain in play until such time as it goes out of play through regular game play. If only one of the game balls gets into play in the top half of the first inning, in the bottom half of the inning, the pitcher must start with the unused ball. No choice is offered.

Otherwise, each pitcher has a choice of game balls at the start of each half inning, but the pitcher may never have possession of both balls at the same time for trial purposes before making a choice. This means that after an inning is completed, the ball should be returned to the vicinity of the pitcher's plate by the team leaving the field or by the umpire. This ensures that the pitcher taking the field has a ball to start the next half inning. The pitcher may request the other ball from the plate umpire prior to the first warm-up pitch. Before the plate umpire relinquishes the second ball, the pitcher must first hand or toss the ball currently in play to the plate umpire. Then, and only then, should the umpire place the second game ball into play. The pitcher has now made a choice and must pitch with that ball.

If the umpire deems any ball unfit, the ball may be replaced without penalty. This ball should be removed from the game permanently.

as some things to keep in mind to help you make a graceful exit. After the final out, give the losing team a reasonable amount of time to make any appeals before you leave the field. After a few minutes, leave the field with the other members of the umpiring crew by exiting on the side where you will receive the least resistance, typically past the winning team's dugout. Important games can become very emotionally charged, so umpires need to remain alert even after the final out.

The plate umpire should return the game balls to the person who provided them. Any significant irregularity or unacceptable conduct should be reported to school administrators and the state association.

Making Your Exit

When leaving the field, be prepared to hear comments and even criticism from coaches, players or fans, often regarding controversial plays. The best way to avoid getting into a discussion with them is to politely say, "I can't discuss the play with you now," or "I can't talk with you now." You have nothing to gain from engaging in conversation about calls that are long over. If someone disagreed with you when the call was made, you won't change the person's mind with a brief discussion after the fact. And more important, what the coach, player or fan believes does not matter. Repeat to yourself, "What the coaches, players and fans believe about calls I made does not matter!" You made the calls as you saw them, and the game is over—that's all that matters. The period from the end of the game to when you actually depart the site can often be the most trying in terms of critical remarks from game participants or spectators. This is a good time to turn your selective hearing filter to its highest setting and keep your eyes straight ahead! Ignore all comments and maintain your composure. To respond or retaliate would be futile and unprofessional, and doing so would damage your standing as a respected authority figure. Once your job is done, be polite to everyone, but quickly leave the area in a professional manner. One final thing to keep in mind if you do hear comments aimed your way is that they are directed at the uniform, not at you personally. Do not take the job home with you—know that you did your best at a difficult job.

Similarly, if you are approached by the media after a game, refer them to the game or tournament administration. Remember that the media make their living by writing stories, especially controversial ones, so make no comments and, above all, keep your cool. Your reputation as an impartial, levelheaded official is your greatest (and most irreplaceable) asset, so be careful with any comments you share. Again, high school softball is a time for student-athletes to shine and enjoy the limelight, not for you to do so. In addition, most state associations have policies regarding speaking to the media.

The Postgame Conference

Get into the habit of gathering with your fellow crew members in a private area away from the field to review the game just completed. Review any unusual situations that occurred during the game and discuss whether the proper call was made. Talk about any breakdowns that occurred in officiating mechanics, what went wrong and how it should be handled next time. Also, go over any rules that you have questions about. This game "postmortem" is an important tool for improving your skills as an umpire and for working on your communication with other officials. The purpose is not to identify who might have made a mistake, but for each member of the crew to learn and become a better umpire. This is a great opportunity to develop collegial friendships with other umpires.

If you study the rules, practice the mechanics and follow the pre- and postgame procedures, you will be well on your way to becoming a good softball umpire. Managing conferences, lineups, appeals and criticism can be nerve-wracking the first few times you are in the hot seat, but you will quickly gain confidence in handling these tasks. The more confident you become, the more you will enjoy being a softball umpire.

PART II

SOFTBALL OFFICIATING MECHANICS

CHAPTER 3

PLATE UMPIRE MECHANICS

As the plate umpire, you are responsible for calling balls, strikes and illegal pitches; ruling on checked swings and appeals; and a great deal more. The plate umpire is involved in nearly every play of the game, so you must stay alert and hustle from beginning to end. Learning and using the proper mechanics will help ensure that you

- know what calls are yours to make,
- are in the right field position to make each call and
- conserve your physical and mental energy so you can maintain focus for the entire game.

Once you know the rules and mechanics, you need to develop your skill at *applying* the rules. The timing of your calls may be the most important of these skills. If you make the call too early, it will appear that you could not have seen the entire play before rendering your judgment. If you make the call too late, players will not have the critical information they need to start their next course of action. In the latter case, you are inhibiting game play rather than making the calls that inform it.

Plate and base umpires alike must develop a consistent rhythm for making calls. Consistency is important because players expect and require calls to be made at a certain point during or after a play. If this moment in time shifts earlier or later relative to the play (a lack of predictable rhythm), the flow of the game will be irregular. For example, if players are accustomed to hearing fairly prompt calls and do not immediately hear a ruling on an overthrow that approached dead-ball territory, they may assume the ball is live when it is not. Extra play might occur defensively and offensively, only to be reversed as a result of a delayed call. Your calls should be made deliberately and consistently only after a play is complete. The only variation in how you make calls should be how emphatic you are with your voice and signaling, depending on the situation. Your sense of timing will become more consistent with experience.

Preparing for the Pitch

Although many of the fundamentals are the same for fast- and slow-pitch softball, there are important differences, particularly in how your body should be positioned just prior to a pitch. A good stance is important for seeing a pitch clearly to determine whether it is a ball or a strike; it will also allow you to move from behind the plate quickly if the ball is hit and to conserve your strength so you can remain alert for the entire game.

Fast Pitch

Prior to the pitch, assume a stance behind the catcher with a line of sight between the batter and the catcher. Your inside ear should be lined up with the inside edge of the plate. This position is called the slot. If you are in the slot, you will be able to see all of home plate and the batter's strike zone, and the catcher can move up and down without obstructing your view. To keep from taxing your back muscles, assume an upright position while waiting for the pitcher and batter to prepare for the pitch. Place your feet at least shoulder-width apart and stand in a relaxed, fully upright position (see figure 3.1). The toe of your slot foot (the foot closest to the batter) should be on a line almost even with the catcher's heels. Your other foot should be behind the catcher with the toe on a line extending from the heel of your slot foot. This foot may be angled slightly to make it easier to drop to a set position.

This stance is referred to as "toe to heel," and it will help you remain balanced and comfortable so you are ready to react to anything that happens. It should be mirrored on both sides of the plate for right- and left-handed batters. This stance will help you conserve energy so you can make it through an entire game without getting fatigued.

Once the batter is set and the pitcher appears ready to pitch, you need to drop to the set position from which you will make your calls. To

FIGURE 3.1   Assuming the upright stance.

drop to the set position, bend your knees comfortably and lean slightly forward at the waist, keeping your back as straight as possible. Your shoulders can be squared with the pitcher or slightly squared with the plate. You should drop to a point where your eyes are approximately at the top of the batter's strike zone. You must be completely dropped and set when the pitch is released. You should never be moving to the set position when the ball is in flight. As with making any call, your view of a play will not be as clear or accurate if your body is in motion.

The timing of dropping to set must be geared to each individual pitcher. As a rule of thumb, the umpire should drop to set just prior to the pitcher's hands separating. If you set too early, your legs and back will get tired, which will cause you to be thinking about your body instead of the pitch. If you set too late, as noted earlier, you are likely to be in motion while the pitch is in the air and will be unable to track the ball in to the plate. Timing is everything.

Your line of sight from the set position should pass unobstructed between the batter and the inside corner of home plate. This is your window on the plate, and it is critical for having a good view of the ball as it passes through or near the strike zone (see figure 3.2). By staggering your position to the side of the catcher and using this "slot window," you will have a clear view of the plate and the batter's strike zone while still allowing the catcher unobstructed move-ment up and down. You should always be able to see the plate and the batter's feet and hands.

The ideal set position for fast-pitch softball is lower than that for slow pitch, although the other position-ing mechanics—visual focus, using the slot and using the upright position to rest— remain the same. For fast pitch, your eyes should be level with the batter's arm-pits in a definite crouched position and they should be looking from slightly outside the strike zone through the entire strike zone.

FIGURE 3.2 Working the slot in the set position.

Your goal should be to maintain a consistent strike zone through-out the game, season and, ultimately, your career as an umpire. Using the proper body positioning consistently for every pitch will help you accomplish this.

Slow Pitch

Working the plate in slow pitch differs from working the plate in fast pitch in a few key ways. First, slow pitch uses a 12-foot maximum and 6-foot minimum pitch height rule, so you need to position yourself to be able to judge the height of the ball and then quickly determine whether the pitch is a ball or strike. Because the speed of the pitch is relatively slow and the ball is considered dead once it is caught by the catcher or hits the ground, you do not have to worry about passed balls, wild pitches or hit batters. Also, there is little danger of batted balls hitting the batter or catcher (or you!), which reduces the chances of injury at the plate. These differences mean you can assume a more relaxed position and devote all your attention to watching the pitcher's delivery and the ball as it approaches home plate.

The overall body positioning for umpiring slow pitch is similar to that for fast pitch, with the same need to see the plate and the batter clearly without being obstructed by or interfering with the catcher. You should have an unimpeded view of the pitcher, the entire strike zone and where the pitch lands or is caught by the catcher. Recall that in slow pitch, any pitched ball that is not hit becomes dead when it touches the ground or the plate.

The main way that slow pitch differs from fast pitch is that you should start in an upright position when the pitcher is about to deliver the ball, as shown in figure 3.1 on page 28. As for how much you bend over or stay upright, keep in mind that it is easier to judge the height of the ball in relation to the 12- and 6-foot limits when you are standing upright versus crouching. Drop to the set position only after you have determined the pitch does not violate either the minimum or maximum height rules. This should be a fluid motion rather than a sudden or jerky one that might throw you off balance. You should be comfortably in the set position when the legal pitch crosses the strike zone.

Generally, for a legal pitch that is close to the *maximum* height, you need to be in a lower set position to best determine if the pitch passes through the strike zone. In other words, start high to judge whether the ball is too high, then bend low to watch the strike zone. Alternatively, you will be better able to judge whether a legal pitch that is close to the *minimum* height passes through the strike zone from a slightly more upright position. This means that you generally do not need to squat as low for a flat pitch as you do for a high-arcing pitch.

If a pitch has been judged illegal, you do not need to drop to the set position; however, if you have already dropped to the set position, you will likely want to stay there until the batter swings or the pitch is complete. In either case, show the delayed dead-ball signal and make the verbal call of "Illegal pitch!" loud enough for the batter and catcher to hear.

Be aware that the catcher does not need to work from the crouch position as in fast pitch, but may be standing up, kneeling on one knee or bent over at the waist. The catcher will generally take a position either directly behind the plate or off to the side of the catcher's box to watch the pitch coming in. The catcher is allowed an 8 1/2-foot-wide space to catch the ball, so the positioning used can vary significantly. As the umpire, you must take care not to interfere with the catcher's movement.

Because the ball is hit and put in play so often in slow-pitch softball, you must always be ready to move out from behind the plate to follow the action, whether trailing a runner to first base or tracking a fly ball. If you leave your position behind home plate to move into the infield, be sure to leave from the left side and carefully avoid the catcher.

Making Calls

As a plate umpire, you will make lots of calls—not only on balls and strikes, but on a variety of other plays. In this section, we'll look at proper mechanics for calling balls, strikes, pitches and outs.

Calling Balls and Strikes

The strike zone for fast pitch is the space above home plate that is between the batter's forward armpit and the top of the knees when the batter assumes a natural batting stance. The strike zone for slow pitch is the space above home plate that is between the batter's highest shoulder and the knees when the batter assumes a natural batting stance. If any part of the ball passes through this zone in flight (except after a bounce), the pitch is a strike. It is up to you to judge what qualifies as the batter's natural batting stance.

Although the strike zones of fast pitch and slow pitch are similar, calling balls and strikes in each presents very different challenges. The arced trajectory of a slow-pitch ball is very different from the fast, flat path of a fast-pitch ball. Similarly, strikeouts occur more frequently in fast pitch and hits more often in slow pitch.

In fast pitch, pitchers must follow several detailed rules to set up and deliver a legal pitch, and your job is to enforce these rules (with help from the base umpires). Fast pitch is aptly named, as pitches can head in your direction at amazingly high speeds. Wearing protective gear is critical to having the confidence and courage to stay focused on the task at hand rather than worrying about injury. Calling slow-pitch balls and strikes might seem easier than fast pitch because the ball is moving more slowly, but it is every bit as challenging for different reasons. Consult the current *NFHS Softball Rules Book* for detailed pitching regulations.

In the event of an illegal pitch, call, "Illegal pitch!" and show the delayed dead-ball signal. An illegal pitch is not considered dead until the end of play action that results from the pitch (thus requiring a delayed dead-ball call and not a dead-ball call). If an illegal pitch occurs on a ball not batted, a ball is added to the pitch count and any base runners are each awarded one base without the risk of being put out. If a called illegal pitch is delivered and the batter hits the ball, at the conclusion of the action, the coach of the team at bat has the choice of accepting the results of the play or the penalty that would have been afforded by the illegal pitch if the batter had not swung and hit the ball.

The keys to calling balls and strikes successfully in fast or slow pitch are consistency and timing.

Working the Plate

The action at home plate is the focus for players, coaches and fans throughout most of the game, and balls and strikes can be a major determinant in which team gets an edge in the competition. Not surprisingly, your actions as plate umpire are under the microscope from beginning to end. Everything we discussed in chapters 1 and 2 in terms of maintaining your authority (without being a dictator), keeping your cool (ignoring critical comments) and making each call *based on the facts of that call only* apply when working the plate. Call pitches as you see them, and keep the game moving.

If you did not see something that a coach is disputing, seek help from a partner who could see the play and change the call, if appropriate. If the call is reversible, do so calmly in a way that preserves your authority. If you feel the dispute is without merit or based solely on judgment, restate your call, briefly explain why you made it (what you saw) and indicate respectfully but with authority that the call is final.

Develop a good, strong voice for calling strikes and a consistent tone for calling balls. Always use the correct signals. Remember, balls are not "no calls." Balls should be called loud enough to be heard by the batter and the catcher. Because no signal is associated with calling a ball, everyone else will know it is a ball when no strike signal is seen. In short, every pitch must be called a strike or a ball, and everyone playing the game should immediately understand what call was made.

Timing Your Call

When you make a pitch call is almost as important as making the *right* pitch call to show both teams that you truly and completely saw the critical movement of the pitch. This was discussed earlier, but it is especially important at the plate. Announcing your call too early creates the appearance that you are guessing. Making your call too late indicates a lack of confidence in your decision. These timing considerations are the same as for making any call in the game, but as the plate umpire, you need to establish a consistent rhythm, as you will likely be making well over 100 pitch calls in a single game. Because you are at the center of the action, you set the tempo of the game more than anyone else. Set a good example for the rest of your crew by calling the plate deliberately and consistently. The standard approach for calling any pitch is as follows:

1. Drop from the upright stance to the set position (remember that fast- and slow-pitch set positions can be different, as described in preceding sections).
2. Allow the pitch to cross home plate.
3. Make the call after the catcher has caught the pitch and not before. Even though your decision is made as the ball crosses home plate, do not make your call until the ball is in the catcher's mitt. This delay is crucial to demonstrate that you have watched the entire pitch and also to avoid distracting the catcher, whose job is not done until the ball is caught. Keep in mind that in slow-pitch softball, if the batter does not hit the ball, the pitch will likely bounce on the ground as opposed to being caught by the catcher. Since there are no wild pitches or steals in slow-pitch softball, all you need to know is that it is OK for this to occur!

If the pitch is a strike, use the following list as a guide for how you should make the call, both verbally and physically:

1. Call, "Strike!" briskly and loudly.
2. Without moving your feet out of your stance, rise to the upright position. It is OK to make the vocal call from the set position so both the catcher and batter can hear it, but your arm signal should be made from the upright position so everyone can see it. Do not move your feet from your original stance position until the signal is complete. Your verbal call should be timed to come shortly after the catcher has caught the ball. Your return to the upright position and your arm signal must occur promptly and fluidly, following your verbal call. Use only one technique throughout the game.

FIGURE 3.3   Calling a strike.

3. To show the strike signal, bring your left hand in toward your body, just above the belt area, and raise your right arm, with the hand open, above your head. Your forearm and upper arm should be at a 90-degree angle or greater. Bring your right forearm forward and slightly downward, as if swinging a hammer, as you close your hand into a fist. This "hammer" signal should not be given until you are in the upright position (see figure 3.3).

4. After making the signal, drop your arms to your sides, step back and relax as you wait for the next pitch. Always watch the pitcher to be sure you begin preparing for the next pitch in plenty of time.

Not every pitch is a strike, of course! Following is the recommended procedure for calling a ball:

1. Follow (track) the ball into the catcher's glove with your nose.

2. Make the crisp verbal call of "Ball!" while still in the set position.

3. Stand, step back and relax as you wait for the next pitch. Watch the pitcher to be sure you are ready for it. Remember, there is no arm signal when calling a ball; there is only a verbal call.

Keep in mind that you are not the on-field announcer or broadcaster for the game, and you should not provide any commentary beyond calling the pitch a ball or a strike. Leave it to the people broadcasting the game to describe the pitches. All you should say as umpire is "Ball!" or "Strike!" ("Ball four!" or "Strike three!" when appropriate) unless asked about a specific pitch. If a coach or player asks where the pitch was located, you can respond.

Keeping the Count

As plate umpire, you are respon-sible for keeping an accurate pitch count throughout the game. Always use the count indicator held in your left hand to be sure you do not lose track of the count. Relay the count periodically by showing the number of balls with your left hand and the number of strikes with your right hand (see figure 3.4). Display the count using consecutive fingers, and show the count to the pitcher in front of and above your body. A closed fist indicates zero. In addition, give the count verbally, always stating the number of balls first and strikes second, such as "Two balls, one strike," not "two-one."

FIGURE 3.4   Showing the count.

How often you provide the count depends on several factors. If the field is equipped with a score-board, you only need to give the count when requested by a player or coach or to correct the scoreboard if it is incorrect. If the scoreboard is incorrect, try to correct it as inconspicuously as possible, as the scorer is also an official of the game and should be treated as an extension of the umpiring team. If there is no scoreboard, the count should be given

- when requested,
- after a delay in the normal flow of the game and
- whenever the next pitch could create a change in the game.

A count of three balls or two strikes on the batter creates a situation where you should announce the count, as the next pitch could result in a walk or a strikeout. Announcing the count at these times alerts the defensive and offensive teams, as well as the umpiring team, to the situation. A final factor that might influence how frequently you provide the count is the level of softball you are umpiring. You generally do not need to announce the count as often at higher levels.

Pitcher and Batter Time Restrictions

Under official rules, a batter has a specific amount of time from when the pitcher receives the ball to enter the batter's box and prepare to hit. A batter can request a time-out, and if you deem the request to be for a legitimate reason, you can grant the time-out by verbally saying, "Time!" and stepping back from the plate. Once the time-out has ended and the ball has been declared live, the time limit for the batter to be ready for the pitch begins anew.

Similarly, the pitcher has time limitations for delivering pitches that you must keep track of. The purpose of these rules is to keep the game moving and to prevent players from delaying the game to gain a competitive advantage. Consult the *NFHS Softball Rules Book* for detailed and current batting and pitching regulations.

Umpiring the Bases

Handling runners on the base paths requires a lot of movement, so this responsibility will test your conditioning more than any other game plays. Many plays will be called at the bases, and depending on the umpiring system in use, you, as the plate umpire, are likely to be involved in quite a bit of on-field action. This is a key reason for knowing where and when to move to ensure being in the right position at the right time.

The golden rule for making calls at the bases is that *no matter where you are, you should always be able to see the critical elements of a play.* This rule should guide your movement and positioning on the field. Position yourself so you can see

- the ball,
- the defensive fielder(s) involved in a play,
- the runner(s) you are responsible for and
- the base where the play is occurring (if applicable).

If you keep these elements in mind when moving to view a play, you will always be in position to make your calls.

Calling Specific Plays

As plate umpire, you have several responsibilities when the batter makes contact with the ball, ranging from catch/no-catch calls on balls hit in the air to fair or foul calls on balls hit near the foul line. As with all aspects of umpiring, you need to work and communicate well with your crewmates to ensure adequate field coverage.

Ten Keys to Successful Plate Umpiring

1. Always hustle to the right position for every call.
2. Communicate with other umpires whenever necessary to clarify play responsibilities.
3. Tell your partners what you are doing, such as "I've got third." Do not tell them what they should do.
4. Never "guess" a player out. If you are not sure, the player is safe. Use your umpiring partners for help if you could not or did not see something clearly—*never* guess.
5. Use an indicator to keep track of balls and strikes, and keep home plate clean so everyone can see it clearly. Carry a pencil and paper to record substitutions and charged conferences—do not rely on your memory.
6. With all calls, use a signal and voice that reflect the importance, difficulty or closeness of a play. "Selling" your call is important to show confidence in your decision.
7. When calling pitches, do not describe the location of the pitch unless asked. A simple "Ball!" or "Strike!" will suffice, or if appropriate, "Ball four!" or "Strike three!" Emphasize the called third strike (a called third strike is always emphasized) to show your confidence in the call, but do so in a reasonable manner that does not intimidate or embarrass the batter. If the batter swings and misses for the third strike, give a nonverbal, routine hammer signal for strike three (in this case, it is obvious to everyone that the batter is out, so there is no point in emphasizing the call).
8. Always use correct and precise hand signals.
9. Always leave your position behind home plate by moving around the catcher and batter to the left side of the plate.
10. Make any dead-ball call immediately to halt game action, thereby avoiding confusion caused by unnecessary continuation of play.

Fly Balls

As the plate umpire, you are responsible for calling all fly balls as fair, foul, out or safe except when a base umpire goes to the outfield to make the call. If a base umpire moves into the outfield on a batted ball, that umpire assumes all responsibility for calling catch/no catch and fair/foul on the play, home run or dead ball. This is an important point to discuss in the pregame umpire's conference, as it is one of the most commonly used of all umpiring mechanics.

FIGURE 3.5   Base umpire calling fair.

A base umpire should only take responsibility for an outfield fly if the ball is hit to a location or in a way that will be difficult for the plate umpire to call. A base umpire who is positioned on the line may go out on a ball near the line that requires a fair/foul ruling (see figure 3.5). This is a judgment call on the part of the base umpire, and it must be made quickly. The base umpire must clearly signal the intent to make the call by moving quickly toward the outfield and by communicating with the plate umpire by calling the plate umpire's name or saying, "Going!" Chapter 5 discusses how different umpiring systems handle special fly-ball situations.

Following are fly-ball situations that may require a base umpire to move into the outfield:

- A sinking line drive or similar hit that the outfielder will need to play near the ground, requiring the umpire to determine if the ball is caught or trapped against the ground. A player traps a ball when it is pinned between the glove and the ground as opposed to catching the ball without letting it touch the ground. A trap is not a catch.
- Some foul balls (depending on the umpiring system in use and the umpire's position).
- A batted ball that is hit near the fence (for example, a ball that might be a home run).
- Two or more fielders converging on the ball.

As a rule of thumb, the plate umpire should *always* plan on making the catch/no-catch and foul/fair call any time the ball is hit out of the infield. The plate umpire must get out as far as possible to get the best look at the play, but he or she should be ready to return quickly to infield duties.

In pursuing fly balls, especially possible trapped balls, do not go directly toward the play. Instead, move in a direction that is parallel to the flight of the ball and provides the best angle for viewing the play (see figure 3.6). The angle at which you view a play is *always* more important than how far you are from the play. You should always come out from behind the plate (by moving around the catcher on the third-base side)

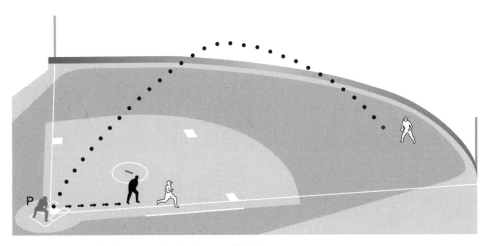

FIGURE 3.6   Calling a play in the outfield.

and move in a direction that will allow you the best view of the outfielder attempting to field the ball. You should move parallel to the path of the hit ball, but keep an eye out for infielders that might obstruct your view and adjust your movement accordingly. Once the play has occurred, give a clear signal and use a loud voice to indicate safe or out.

Fair and Foul Balls

On fly balls hit near the foul lines, your first priority is always to determine whether the ball is fair or foul. To make this judgment most credible, you should always try to straddle the line to make fair/foul calls. Your next priority is to call the batter out or safe.

Consider the consequences of a routine fly ball hit down the line that everyone expects to be caught, but that is dropped. Everyone immediately knows that the batter is safe, but without your call of fair or foul, no one knows whether the ball is live or dead! Should the runners try to advance, or are they required to stay where they are? Make the fair or foul call as soon as it can be determined. You do not need to make a call on any batted ball that is obviously fair or foul (but you do need to call out or safe in the event of a catch attempt).

Batted balls hit near foul lines should be called fair or foul when the status is determined prior to a catch. Make a decisive call as follows:

- On all foul balls (except a caught fly ball that is foul), give the foul ball signal and call, "Foul ball!"
- On all caught fly balls that are foul, the ball remains live and requires only the "Out!" call.
- On any bobbled ball (not caught simultaneously with the first touching of the ball) over foul territory, extend the arm nearest foul

territory horizontally out from your body. If the ball is subsequently caught, signal and call, "Out!" If the ball is not caught, signal and call, "Foul ball!"

You do not need to signal or voice any call for an obviously fair ball if it is obviously not caught. In other words, for fly balls, you only need to make a fair or foul call on uncaught balls close to the line and bobbled fair balls. Every caught fly requires an out signal. Fair balls are never verbalized; they are only signaled.

Batted balls hit out of the park near the foul lines should also be called very decisively as either a home run or foul ball so there can be no question about your decision on the play. When a ball is hit deep into the outfield, you should not judge the ball to be fair or foul until it passes the outfield fence or barrier. Wind can change the course of long fly balls, so to be safe, wait until the ball is *clearly* either fair or foul.

Finally, as plate umpire, you are responsible for calling fair or foul on all batted balls that pass near or over first or third base, regardless of whether a base umpire is positioned on the foul line. To sum it all up, you need to stay on your toes because the plate umpire is responsible for nearly all batted balls!

Home Runs

One of the most exciting moments in softball is when a well-hit ball travels over the outfield fence in fair territory. Players, coaches and fans will jump out of their seats to celebrate the towering hit, but you need to remain focused and keep the game under control. Players should not be allowed to run onto the field to meet the batter between third base and home plate or any time before all bases have been touched. If they begin to do so, motion them back and tell them to stay back until the batter touches the plate. Do not allow them to obstruct your view of the runner(s) touching the plate. Once the batter has touched the plate, it is acceptable for teammates to join the batter at the plate *briefly* to celebrate the accomplishment.

As soon as the batter passes third base (and not before), take the next game ball out of your ball bag. As soon as the batter touches home plate, give the ball to the catcher or pitcher. Next, move so you are facing the backstop in front of the plate and quickly dust off home plate, then return to your position behind the catcher by moving through the batter's box opposite the next batter. Home runs are exciting, but they should not compromise the pace or your control of the game.

Keep in mind that in slow pitch, if an outfielder touches a fly ball that subsequently goes over the fence in fair territory, the hit is considered a four-base award rather than a home run. Your job as umpire in this situation is similar to that of signaling a home run except you raise four fingers over your head (rather than using the closed-fist signal for a home run) and give a verbal call ruling a four-base award.

Trailing the Batter-Runner Toward First Base

One of the plate umpire's duties is to be in a good position to assist (if requested) the base umpire with various aspects of an initial play at first base on the batter-runner. Following are aspects of the play that a base umpire may need help with:

1. Tags made by the catcher or any infielder on the batter-runner. This play is the responsibility of the plate umpire when it occurs prior to the 3-foot running lane.
2. Violations of the 3-foot running lane.
3. Overthrows and blocked balls.
4. Questions of whether the first-base fielder's foot was pulled from the base.
5. Questions of whether the first-base fielder has possession of the ball.

To fulfill this responsibility with no runners on or only a runner on first, the plate umpire should exit the plate area to the left of the catcher, move quickly toward the first-base foul line, remain in fair territory and follow (trail) the batter-runner, coming to a stop no more than halfway down the line to observe the play (see figure 3.7).

Always leave the plate area to the left of the catcher because the catcher will generally move directly toward first base to back up a play there and the batter-runner always heads toward first. This will help you avoid colliding with the catcher or runner, something you definitely do not want to happen.

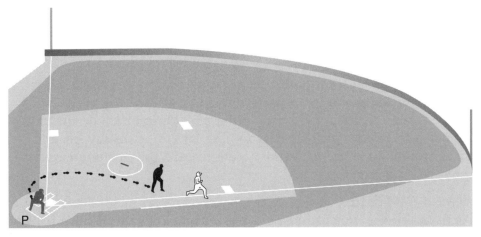

FIGURE 3.7   Trailing the runner.

If there is a runner on first, you are responsible for any play at third base (in the two-umpire system) if the runner advances that far. In this case, begin your movement toward first base, but only traverse one-third of the distance to first. After the play at first, quickly change direction and head diagonally toward the third-base foul line. From the line, move as close to the base as you can before having to stop and make the call (see figure 3.8). This approach allows you to establish your best angle first and then close the distance if possible. The key is to prepare to make or assist with a call on the batter-runner but keep track of the lead runner and then quickly get in position to have a good angle for a play at third.

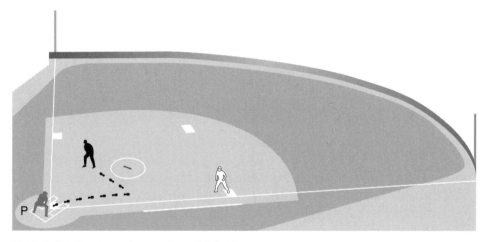

FIGURE 3.8   Covering a play at third base.

If there are runners beyond first base and the initial play will be at first, you still have the trail responsibilities, but you cannot trail the batter-runner, as you would risk putting the action behind your back. In these cases, you should drop back to a position on the first-base line extended in foul territory. From this position, you have the same angle to observe the play at first base as trailing the batter-runner gave you, yet are open to see all other action on the field. If there is a subsequent play at the plate or third base, you are in a position to see it developing and can quickly move into a correct position.

Do not trail if there will be no initial play at first base on the batter-runner. If there is no play, there is nothing for you to assist with. In these cases, move out from behind the plate toward the pitching circle and move as the action indicates.

Plays at Third Base

As plate umpire, you are responsible for making calls at third base in all umpire systems. To do so, leave your position behind the plate and move approximately halfway toward third base in foul territory while watching the play develop. If a call has to be made at third base, cut inside the diamond (see figure 3.9) about two-thirds of the way to third, then move to within 10 to 12 feet of the base to make the call.

You should be inside the diamond at this point because this position will give you the best angle to make the call. If the ball gets away from the third-base player, it is likely to go into foul territory, which means you are already out of the way. Similarly, if the runner continues to advance around third toward home, you are less likely to collide with the runner if you are inside the diamond and are in an excellent position to move back down the line in fair territory to make a call at home plate.

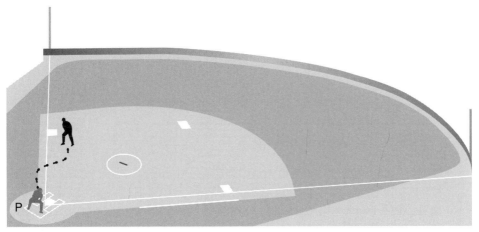

FIGURE 3.9   Moving from home plate to make a call at third base.

Rundowns

A rundown occurs when a runner is trapped between bases (with no force in effect) and two or more defensive players attempt to tag the runner out. Rundowns typically occur without much warning, so a single umpire often covers both ends of the play. However, if another umpire is in position to help, the two of you need to team up to cover both ends of the play. Always be alert for possible obstruction during a rundown.

If you are covering a rundown by yourself, move quickly to be in the best position to view both ends of the rundown where the final play might occur. Position yourself a minimum of 12 feet from the runner and move parallel to the base path the runner is on. You need not mirror the runner's entire movement back and forth, but you must hustle enough to have a good perspective at whichever end the play finally takes place. If a partner arrives to help, neither of you needs to move with the rundown, as both ends will be covered. A note of warning: Make no assumptions about where the play is going to end, as defensive errors can change the outcome of a rundown very quickly. When the actual tag is attempted, move quickly toward or around the play to get the best angle and make your call with confidence.

If two umpires are in position to handle a rundown together, they should bracket the play, with one umpire taking a position ahead of the runner and the other umpire staying behind the runner. The umpires should be on opposite sides of the base path, but this is not always possible. Communication is essential whenever two umpires team up to call a play. The umpire taking the position ahead of the base runner should say, "I've got the lead," or "I've got this end!" Similarly, the umpire in the rear position should do the same so there is no question about how the play is being handled. This communication will help avoid situations where neither umpire is moving into position to make the call or where both umpires are prepared to make the call (and potentially not the same call!). When two umpires are covering a rundown, the direction in which the runner is moving at the time of the tag dictates which umpire makes the call. In other words, if the runner is moving toward you, you make the call. If the runner is moving away from you, your partner should make the call.

Following are a few of the most common rundown scenarios (depending on the number of base umpires):

- If the runner is between first and second base, the plate umpire should take the trail position, near first base. The base umpire should take the lead position, close to second base. The plate umpire should be inside the diamond and the base umpire outside the diamond.

- If the lead runner is between second and third base, the plate umpire should take the lead position closest to third base, inside the diamond, and the base umpire should take the trail position closest to second base, on the outfield side of the diamond.

- If the rundown is between third base and home plate, the plate umpire should take the lead position nearest home plate, outside the diamond, and the base umpire should take the trail position near third base, inside the diamond (see figure 3.10).

Tag Plays at the Plate

For making calls on tag plays at the plate, you should be in one of three positions, depending on where you are positioned before the play develops and how the play is developing:

1. On plays where the ball is coming from fair territory (for example, a throw from the center fielder), you should assume a position in foul territory at a 90-degree angle to the path of the runner and 10 to 12 feet from home plate (see figure 3.11). This is the most com-

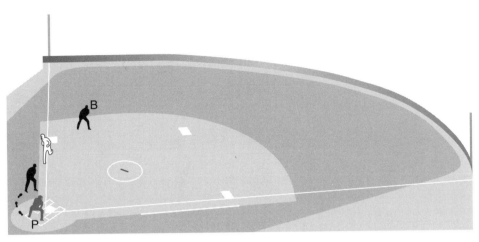

FIGURE 3.10   Covering a rundown between third base and home plate.

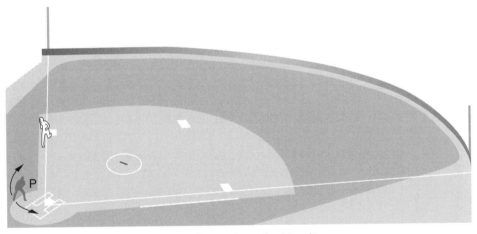

FIGURE 3.11   Calling a play at home from foul territory.

mon (default) position for most plays at the plate. After making the call, you need to clear out while continuing to watch the ball, always remaining in foul territory.

2. If you are inside the diamond, returning from third base, move toward home plate parallel to the third-base line and assume a position 10 to 12 feet from the plate and at a 90-degree angle to the path of the runner (see figure 3.12). Keep your weight distributed on the balls of your feet so you can move quickly if your view is suddenly obstructed by a slide or a shift in position by the catcher. Move in on the play as it develops, find the ball and make the call.

3. On plays where the throw pulls the catcher up the third-base line and away from the plate, making a swiping tag highly probable, you

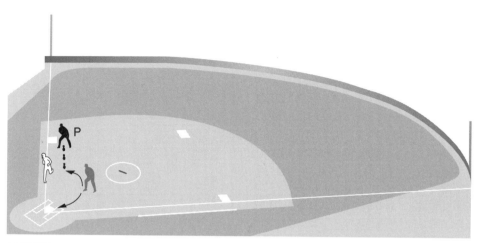

FIGURE 3.12 Moving from third base to make a call at home plate.

should take a position on the third-base line extended in foul territory. This gives you the best angle to see the tag applied. Do not attempt to use this position if the play will involve the runner attempting to touch the plate. If the plate is involved, you must be able to see the front of the plate and have a straight-line view down onto the play so you can judge when the runner reaches the plate. It is rare, and often impossible, for an umpire to be able to use this position in the two-umpire system because the plate umpire almost always has responsibilities at third base and is not able to get to the plate in time. In these cases, use the default position but move in to see the tag.

Because plays at the plate are especially important, you need to be more aggressive in preparing for and making calls. For a tag play at the plate, quickly move in close to the play and visually locate the ball. If you cannot find it, ask the player to show you the ball to demonstrate possession. If the defensive player made the out, point at the ball with your left hand and "sell" your call with your right-hand out signal as well as a strong verbal call. Calls at the plate require more emphasis because a run is at stake.

Be especially alert for defensive obstruction when watching plays at the plate. Obstruction occurs when a defensive player impedes the progress of a runner (e.g., by blocking the base without the ball) who is legally running bases. (Note: It is also obstruction if a defensive player interferes with a batter's attempt to make contact with a pitched ball.) The interfering act may be intentional or unintentional, physical or verbal. It is not obstruction if the fielder has the ball, is about to receive the ball or is fielding a batted ball.

Appeal at the Plate

If a runner misses home plate and the catcher misses the tag, the umpire should hesitate slightly to allow the players to finish the play—either the runner reaches to tag the plate or the catcher reaches to tag the runner. If no tag is made and all players continue unknowingly, the runner should be considered safe. However, if the fielder makes a proper appeal by touching either the runner or the plate with the ball prior to the runner touching the plate, then you should declare the runner out.

This procedure makes sense for three reasons:

1. The missed tag is a play, and it is the umpire's job to rule on plays.
2. A runner is assumed to be safe until put out.
3. If a runner advances beyond a base, she is assumed to have touched it unless an appeal is made to the umpire.

Timing Play

In situations where the precise timing of a tag out determines whether or not a runner crossing the plate has scored, the umpire calling the tag out must call the play loudly the moment it occurs so the plate umpire can judge whether the lead runner has touched the plate before (the run counts) or after (the run does not count) the tag out. Generally, umpires should briefly delay announcing a call to ensure that the play is completely over, but this situation is different and requires the tag play to be called without any delay. The plate umpire should immediately and without hesitation state that the "Run counts!" or the "Run does not count!" and should inform the scorekeeper as appropriate.

A run does not count if the third out of the inning is the result of

- a batter-runner being put out prior to reaching first base;
- any force-out—including an appeal at a base to which the runner was forced at the time of the infraction;
- an appeal at a base to which a runner was forced to advance;
- a runner being put out by a tag or live-ball appeal play prior to the lead runner touching home plate or
- a preceding runner (who appeared to have scored) is declared out on an appeal play.

Note that an appeal can be made after the third out, and if legitimate, it could nullify a run.

Calling Special Situations at the Plate

As if calling balls and strikes, batted balls and close plays on the base paths were not enough, you need to be ready for several additional situations at the plate. Take heart, however, as all the basic principles of effective umpiring—knowing where the ball is, moving to get a good viewing angle, "selling" the call with confidence and always keeping your composure—apply to these special situations.

Passed Balls and Pop Flies to the Screen

If a pitch gets by the catcher (a passed ball or wild pitch, depending on whether the pitcher or catcher is at fault) (fast pitch only) or the batted ball is popped up backward toward the screen (fast and slow pitch), your first priority is to get out of the way of the catcher. Move away from the catcher as quickly as possible to avoid interfering with retrieval of the ball or a collision with the catcher. To do this, back away from the catcher as you remove your mask, watching the catcher carefully. The catcher's shoulders will indicate the likely direction of movement, which should tell you the direction to move to avoid getting in the way. Once you have started getting out of the catcher's way, locate the ball. This will help you anticipate how the play will develop and will also help you remain out of the catcher's path.

On a pop-up, you must watch the backstop and the foul line. If the batted ball goes back to the screen, follow the play to the fence to observe a possible trap against the screen, the ball becoming blocked (for example, stuck in the fence) or the ball leaving the field of play (a dead-ball situation). If the pop fly is near the foul line, remember that your first priority is to decide if it is fair or foul, then out or safe.

If there is a runner at third base, be aware that there could be a play at the plate on a pop-up, and in fast pitch, a steal, a passed ball or wild pitch.

No matter where you move to establish your angle of view on the play, always know where the ball is—there will not be a close play without it!

Illegal Pitches

Plate and base umpires each have different responsibilities for calling illegal pitches. Each umpire has a unique viewing angle of the pitcher and thus may see rule infractions the other umpire cannot. The following sections discuss the mechanics that dictate which umpire should make the different types of calls. Consult the *NFHS Softball Rules Book* for detailed pitching rules.

Generally, the plate umpire should look for and call pitching violations involving

- time restrictions (for example, the pitcher takes longer than the allotted time before pitching the ball);
- the width of the 24-inch pitching plate (fast pitch only);
- the delivery, such as sidearm, three-quarters or overarm and
- anything to do with the hands.

The base umpire should look for and call pitching violations involving

- the pivot foot on the pitching plate,
- a backward step of the non-pivot foot,
- use of a "crow hop" (lifting and replanting of the pivot foot prior to starting the pitch) and
- use of a "leap" (both of the pitcher's feet leave the ground prior to delivering the pitch).

The illegal pitch needs to be called the moment it becomes illegal. However, the illegal pitch call is always a delayed dead-ball call and should only be loud enough to be heard by the nearest fielder (if by a base umpire) or the catcher and batter (if by the plate umpire) so that the batter still has the choice of swinging at the pitch.

To call an illegal pitch, use the delayed dead-ball signal and call, "Illegal pitch!" Do not call time until the pitch has reached the catcher or the play on a batted ball has been completed.

Dead Balls

Several special occurrences create a dead-ball situation:

- *Batter hit by pitch.* In fast pitch, if a pitched ball hits a batter, the batter is awarded first base as long as
  - the batter makes an attempt to avoid the pitch,
  - the batter does not swing and
  - the pitch is not in the strike zone.

  Keep in mind that, contrary to a popular but incorrect belief, the hands are not considered part of the bat. Any time the batter is hit by a pitched ball, the ball is dead. In slow-pitch softball, the ball is also dead, but no awards are granted.

- *Batter hits the ball twice with the bat.* When considering the act of a batter hitting the ball a second time, the umpire should categorize the act in one of three ways:
  1. If the bat is in the batter's hands when the ball comes in contact with it the second time, and the batter is in the batter's box, it is a foul ball. If one of the batter's feet is entirely outside the

batter's box, the batter is out. When in doubt, don't "guess" the batter out. Call it foul.

2. If the bat is out of the batter's hands (dropped or thrown) and the ball and bat come in contact with each other a second time, the ball remains live and would be fair or foul depending on its location when touched by a player or when it comes to rest in relation to the foul line. It makes no difference if the bat hits the ball or the ball hits the bat. If the ball and bat come in contact with each other a second time in foul territory, the ball is foul. However, if the batter intentionally hits the ball a second time, the ball is dead, the batter is out and all runners must return to the base they occupied at the time of the pitch.

3. If a batter swings and misses the pitched ball but accidentally hits it on the follow-through, intentionally hits it on the second swing or hits it after it bounces off the catcher or her glove, the ball is dead and all runners must return to the base they occupied prior to the pitch. If the act is intentional with runner(s) on base, the batter is called out for interference.

- *Batted ball hits the batter.* If a batted ball is over fair territory when it hits the batter's body, the batter is out unless she is in the batter's box (including the portion of the batter's box in fair territory). If the ball is over foul territory when it hits the batter, it is a foul ball. This play is often difficult to see well because the catcher may obstruct your view or the ball may hit the batter out in front where it cannot be seen from behind the plate. This situation underscores the importance of the plate umpire having the support of the base umpire(s). The base umpires should be ready to make this call if the plate umpire cannot.

  This play can be a prime cause for embarrassment if umpires do not work together as a team. If the ball is hit off the batter's foot and rolls into fair territory (and thus appears to be a fair hit), it will be obvious to many that it should be called a dead ball. Because of your more obscured view, it is difficult to call and can quickly lead to controversy. You should cover this point with all umpires in the pregame conference to make sure your partners are watching carefully and are ready to help throughout the game.

  This initial dead-ball call can be made by either the plate or base umpire(s), but the penalty must be determined by the plate umpire. The batter gets the benefit of the doubt unless circumstances preclude the ball being called foul.

- *Catcher obstruction.* Catcher obstruction occurs when the catcher hinders or prevents a batter from swinging at a pitched ball (for example, the catcher's glove makes contact with the batter's bat during a swing). Catcher obstruction can occur on either the forward or backward swing of the batter, and the call is a delayed dead-ball signal. If the batter hits the ball and advances one base, and all other runners advance one base, the obstruction is ignored and no award or penalty is issued. If the batter and all other runners do not advance one base, the offensive coach is given the option of taking the result of the play or the award for catcher obstruction where the batter is awarded first base and other runners advance only if forced.

If the obstruction occurs prior to the pitch being released, call, "Dead ball!" immediately, then move around to the front of the plate and clean it, giving both the batter and catcher time to reset. While doing this, instruct the catcher not to obstruct the batter, and then resume play. Even though catcher obstruction is usually accidental on the part of the catcher, it must be called because it disadvantages the batter.

Checked Swings

The checked swing is one of the toughest situations to handle as a plate umpire. A checked swing occurs when a batter halts the progress of the bat in midswing without hitting the ball. Essentially, you need to determine two things at once:

1. Was the pitch a strike? If so, it does not matter whether or not the batter swung—it is a strike either way.
2. If the pitch was a ball, did the batter swing the bat past the point of commitment as determined in the *NFHS Softball Rules Book*, thereby requiring a strike call?

This call is yours to make as the plate umpire; however, if the pitch is not in the zone and you are in doubt about whether the batter swung, you should immediately ask for help from the base umpire, who has a different, and in some ways better, angle to determine how far the bat was swung. If you call the pitch a ball and the catcher asks you to seek an opinion from a base umpire, do it. If you call the pitch a strike, either because it was in the zone or you judged the batter to have swung, there is no need to seek an opinion from a base umpire. Once a strike is called, it remains a strike. Keep in mind that asking for help from a base umpire on a checked swing is not a sign of inability. The pitch is your primary call; the swing of the bat is a secondary call. It also shows you are more concerned with getting the call right than with how you are perceived, a sign of a conscientious umpire. Umpires are encouraged to always seek help on checked swings when requested to do so.

To ask for help, remove your mask, step out from behind the catcher and point to your umpiring partner closest to the foul line away from the batter.

For right-handed batters, this is the umpire closest to the first-base line. For left-handed batters, it is the umpire closest to the third-base line.

Following are four points to consider in determining whether a batter swung the bat or checked the swing:

1. Did the batter's wrist roll or break?
2. Did the batter swing through the ball? If the batter pulled the bat back *after* the plane of the bat crossed the plane of the ball, it should be considered a swing and thus a strike. If the batter pulled the bat back before the bat crossed the plane of the ball, it should be considered a checked swing and thus a ball.
3. Did the batter swing far enough that the bat was out in front of the batter?
4. Did the batter make an attempt to hit the pitch?

You will want to modify your mechanics to make it clear that you called a strike because the batter swung, not because of the pitch's location. This prevents game participants from interpreting the strike call as just a bad call. If a pitch is *obviously* a ball and the player tried unsuccessfully to check the swing, stand and point at the batter (use your left hand for right-handed batters and your right hand for left-handed batters), say, "Swing," then give the strike signal. Make it clear to all that you called a strike because the batter swung at the pitch.

If the plate umpire asks for help, the base umpire should respond by saying, "Yes" and giving an out signal or "No" and giving a safe signal. The plate umpire does not need to echo the call, but should give the count before the next pitch so everyone knows what the previous pitch was ruled.

Time-Outs and Suspension of Play

There are situations where you, as the plate umpire, need to call a time-out to suspend game play. These include legitimately requested batter time-outs, injuries, substitutions, distractions on the field or any number of other interruptions.

To call a time-out properly, extend both hands, with palms open and facing forward, high above your head and angled slightly outward, while making a verbal call of "Time out!" (see figure 3.13). Be sure to make the call loudly and clearly so everyone knows play is dead. Play is resumed with a distinct "Play ball!" call (see figure 3.14).

To instruct the pitcher not to pitch, show the "hold play" signal to the pitcher by extending your arm straight forward with the hand pulled up, exposing the palm to the pitcher (see figure 3.15). Use your right arm for right-handed batters and your left arm for left-handed batters. The ball is dead at this time, and if the pitcher delivers a pitch while you are holding play, a "no pitch" should be declared.

FIGURE 3.13 Calling a time-out.

FIGURE 3.14 Giving a play ball signal.

FIGURE 3.15 Giving a do not pitch ("hold play") signal.

If a batter has one foot in the batter's box and one foot out, the batter is not ready for a pitch to be thrown. In this case, hold up play by using your "do not pitch" signal, if necessary. If the batter has both feet in the batter's box, the batter should request a time-out before stepping out. If the pitcher has already started the pitch, then a time-out should not be granted and play should continue.

Conferences

When playing defense, each team is allowed three "charged" or official conferences during a seven-inning game (with additional conferences provided for extra innings; consult the *NFHS Softball Rules Book* for specific regulations). Offensive teams are allowed one conference per inning for coaches to confer with batters or base runners (again, refer to the *NFHS Softball Rules Book* for current rules). It is the plate umpire's responsibility to enforce the rules governing conferences, which generally come down to

- acknowledging requests for conferences,
- judging whether a conference has occurred, even if it was not requested, and
- keeping track of the number of conferences (write it down to avoid any question).

If a charged conference must be assessed, you need to inform the team being charged that a conference has been assessed by saying, "That is a charged conference."

Following are a few points to remember about conferences:

- An offensive conference may include the batter or any number of runners, players or coaches.
- A defensive conference is charged only when the coach or other team representative from the dugout requests (and is granted) time to confer with a player or players. Providing instruction from the dugout area is not considered a conference. Also, conferences among players on the field, such as the pitcher and catcher, are not charged conferences because no bench/dugout personnel are involved.
- When either team is involved in a charged conference, the other team may also have a conference that is not charged, provided the noncharged conference concludes when the opposing team's charged conference ends, thus not delaying the game. Once the umpire instructs the team that is charged with the conference to play ball, both teams must immediately resume play or be in jeopardy of having a conference assessed to them.

CHAPTER 4

BASE UMPIRE MECHANICS

Like the plate umpire, the base umpire must keep track of many game elements in order to react correctly to every play. Where you stand and what you do when a play begins depends on how many umpires you are working with and where runners are located. Although field positioning is different for two- and three-umpire systems, the basic principles are the same. The two-umpire system is the primary system referred to throughout this chapter. A few key differences in base umpire responsibilities between fast- and slow-pitch softball are highlighted in this chapter and in chapter 5.

As a base umpire, you should be responsible for

- calling plays at or between bases,
- covering plays in the outfield that would be too difficult for the plate umpire to see,
- watching for illegal pitches,
- watching the batter for possible checked swings and
- knowing the game situation at all times to assist other umpires.

As a base umpire, you need to be ready for every play before it occurs. In addition, plays or other situations requiring your involvement can develop between pitches or between innings, so you must stay focused and alert throughout the entire game. Additionally, communication is also critical to your success; use voice and eye contact to convey your intentions and to let others know you are tuned in to the game.

Preplay Preparation

Where you move and what you are looking for depends on the current game situation, so you need to be aware of certain game information at all times. Before every pitch, mentally review your game situation checklist and action plan, as provided on page 56. This exercise is especially helpful if you are new to umpiring, and it continues to be important no matter how many games you have umpired. After a while this review will become automatic, and you will instinctively know the action plan.

Game Situation Checklist

___ **How many outs are there?**
- Play may remain live if the defensive team makes a single out versus if there are two outs before play begins.
- More emphasis on a call may be in order for the third out.
- There could be a tag-up situation if a runner is on and there are fewer than two outs.

___ **What is the count?**
- More emphasis on a call may be in order if called upon to rule on a checked swing that creates the third strike.
- Runners are likely to take certain actions depending on the count.

___ **How many runners are on? Where? Who are you responsible for?**
- Determines which runner(s) you need to watch.
- Informs you where the next play is likely to be.
- Prepares you for a force play versus a tag play.

___ **What does the game situation suggest the batting team will do?**
- In a sacrifice, the batter may be more likely to attempt a bunt.
- Certain game situations make a steal more likely.
- Watch for hit-and-run situations where the runner will be leaving the base early, expecting the batter to hit the ball.

___ **What is the score of the game?**
- It is important to be aware of the score in case asked by a player; and the closer the game, the more you need to be on top of things and "sell" your calls effectively.
- Expect to get more "flack" late in a close game.
- With a tied score or a one-run difference, prepare for a squeeze play.
- Expect sloppy play in a lopsided game and stay focused.

___ **Where does the batter usually hit the ball? Is the batter a power or contact hitter?**
- Track batter tendencies to help you create your action plan.
- If a batter tends to hit the ball to the outfield, you can prepare for likely events in terms of runners, tag-ups covering a defensive play in the outfield.

___ **How are the fielders set up?**
- Be aware of any defensive shifts to anticipate plays.

___ **How is the defensive team pitching the batter?**
- Outside pitches tend to be hit away from the batter and inside pitches are more likely to be pulled toward the batter.

From *Officiating Softball* by ASEP, 2004, Champaign, IL: Human Kinetics.

Until this analysis becomes instinctive, you should take a moment before each pitch to get everything straight in your mind. Just as the players need to know the game situation, so do you. If you played the sport before becoming an umpire, you should already have a feel for the game. However, whether or not you are a former player, be sure to run through your mental checklist before each play.

Body Position

Umpires use two primary body positions while in the field—the upright and the set position (see figures 4.1 and 4.2). The set position can be broken down into a full set—hands on knees—or a standing ready set—standing, slightly bent, hands in fists pulled into the hipbone/groin area. Generally, you should stand in the upright position when there are no runners on base and the set position when there are runners on base.

The upright position is more comfortable and uses less energy, helping you save strength to make it through to the final batter. The set position allows you to react and move more quickly to cover bases when runners are on the move. However, even in the upright position, you should be balanced on both feet and ready to move—you never know when you might need to really hustle to cover a surprise play! Also, do not fold

FIGURE 4.1 Assuming an upright position.

FIGURE 4.2 Assuming a set position.

your arms across your chest or put your hands on your hips. Always keep your arms at your sides. Folding your arms conveys the impression of arrogance and defensiveness.

As the pitcher begins the pitching motion, the base umpire should be in an upright, ready position, with weight evenly distributed on the balls of the feet. This will help you move more quickly when a play begins. It also shows everyone in the game that you are focused and alert and will help prevent pulled muscles or other injuries.

Positioning on the Field

Where you stand prior to a pitch depends on how many base umpires there are and which bases have runners. Chapter 5 provides detailed blueprints for different umpiring systems (one, two or three umpires) and game situations, but there are a few rules of thumb for base umpires that are universal. These positioning and movement "rules" will help you know whether you should be inside or outside the diamond and whether you should be in fair or foul territory.

Plays in the Infield

The key positioning considerations for balls hit in the infield are

- whether you should be positioned in the infield or the outfield side of the diamond and
- whether you should be in fair or foul territory.

Inside-Outside

The inside-outside rule dictates whether you should move inside the bases or stay on the outfield side of the diamond, depending on where the ball is located and where the play is happening. This approach applies to both fast- and slow-pitch softball and to two-, three- or four-umpire systems.

If the ball is hit inside the diamond (a fair ball in the infield), you should move into fair territory on the outfield side of the diamond to be sure you have a good view of all the key elements of the play. In this case, your back is to the outfield and you are looking toward home plate through the infield (see figure 4.3).

If the ball is hit to the outfield, you should move inside the diamond, turning as necessary to keep the ball in view, as shown in figure 4.4.

When moving from outside to inside the diamond, you should use the "buttonhook" maneuver to get into position. This maneuver allows you to move quickly—you want to be turned and in position before the runner gets to the base—to the spot you need to be in, minimizing the amount of time your back is turned to the play. Once you are 10 to 12 feet past the baseline, pivot (or buttonhook) into the play to get the best

FIGURE 4.3   Moving to cover a ball hit to the infield.

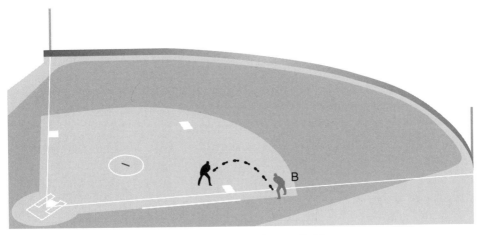

FIGURE 4.4   Moving to cover a ball hit to the outfield.

view possible (see figure 4.5). The buttonhook could also be thought of as a J-pattern, leaving you in a good position to see the runner touch the base and to move with the runner in either advancing or retreating.

As you move toward the inside of the diamond, you should be watching the ball and the runner(s) you are responsible for. What happens with the ball dictates your next play, so you must always keep an eye on the ball. Obstruction can happen without the ball, and you can watch for it by periodically glancing at the runner(s) as you hustle inside.

Wherever the ball is hit, you should always seek a position that enables you to see the following elements:

- The ball
- The runner(s) you are responsible for

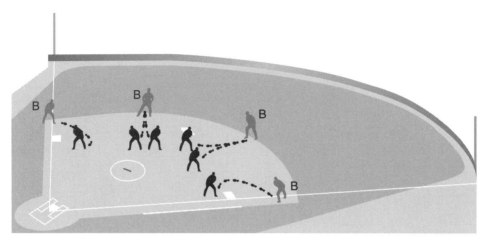

FIGURE 4.5   Using the buttonhook movement pattern.

- The defensive player(s) involved in a play (infield and outfield)
- The base you are covering

The Pitch

With no runners on base, you will be 15 to 18 feet down the line in foul territory in the upright position. Watch the pitcher's feet for legality and begin to take a step (still watching the pitcher) as the pitcher begins the windup. If the pitcher's footwork is legal, when the ball is released, shift your eyes to the batter as you complete your second step, ending in a balanced stance with your weight on both feet, able to move in any direction. If the ball is not hit, follow it on in to the catcher's mitt and prepare to move back to your original position.

This technique will help prevent pulled muscles or other injuries resulting from sudden or late starts. More important, it directs your eyes to what you must see—the pitcher's feet, then anything at the plate your partner may need help with—and leaves you ready to move.

Fair/Foul Territory

If your starting position is in foul territory, move into fair territory on any ground balls hit to the infield. Move into fair territory so the corner of the outfield side of first base is pointing at you—approximately 90 degrees to the path of the ball—and stay at least 15 to 18 feet from the base (see figure 4.6). As you are moving, watch the defensive player fielding the ball. Stop, watch the fielder release the throw, then follow the flight of the ball from the fielder's hand to the base you are covering, while turning your body toward the base and dropping to a set position. When you have determined the throw is on target (not wild or overthrown) and it is about halfway to the base, shift your eyes to the receiver's glove to watch the catch. The throw should guide your sightline and body angle into the play.

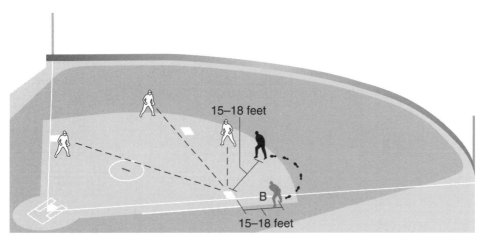

FIGURE 4.6 Moving to fair territory on ground balls to the infield.

If you are the first-base umpire with a runner on first base and need to cover a possible double play, take one step toward second base to get a better view of the defensive turn at second (did the fielder have possession of the ball when touching the base?), and then quickly move toward first base to get the same angle on the play as you would if you were coming off the line. Do not take your eye off the ball, as it may take too long to find it again. Then let the flight of the ball direct your head and body angle into the play at first base, making sure you are positioned to see the fielder's foot, the runner's foot and the fielder's glove. Calling the out on the front end of a double play is one of the rare cases where it is OK for an umpire to be moving while signaling a call.

If there is a bobble at second base or the runner is safe, a play at first base is unlikely. In this case, continue to move in on the play at second base.

Exceptions to this "fair territory" rule are if the ball is hit to the second-base fielder's far left or if she is moving to her left to field the ball. You cannot move into fair territory at risk of interfering with the play. Also, on sharply hit balls to right field where there may be a play on the batter-runner at first base, you may not have time to get into the baseline (your preferred position), especially if you must hesitate to see if the second-base fielder might knock down the ball. In these cases, you will need to take a position in foul territory. Do not move up the line or go beyond a 45-degree angle off the line, as this will obscure your view of the elements of the play—the right fielder, the ball, the runner and first base. Maintain a distance of 15 to 18 feet and watch the play develop using the techniques described previously (see figure 4.7).

Avoid getting too close to the action. You need to be able to see the fielder's foot on the base (usually the edge nearest the ball), the runner's foot touching the base (always a different edge than where the fielder's

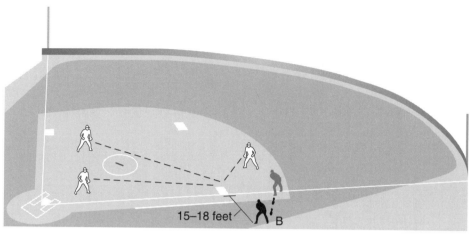

FIGURE 4.7   Calling a play at first base from foul territory.

foot touched) and the fielder catching the ball (possibly above her head and definitely some distance from her foot).

The disadvantage of calling plays from foul territory is that it puts you behind the runner if the play does not end at first base (due to an overthrow or error), thus allowing the runner to attempt to advance. The only thing you can do is run as hard as you can to get the best angle possible for the play at second. Remember that your angle of view is far more important than your distance from the play. Be sure to keep your eye on the ball as you move toward second.

Finally, when moving into foul territory, you may need to ask the base coach to clear the area for you. This is within your authority. Never allow a coach to be between you and the play.

For all these reasons, try to make first-base calls from fair territory unless the game situation forces you to move. If you do move into foul territory, reestablish a more desirable position as soon as you can. In the three-umpire system, it is acceptable and often preferred for you to be in foul territory, since the umpire making a call at third has no previous or future bases to cover.

Plays in the Outfield

The core umpiring principle of keeping all game elements in view also applies if a ball is hit to the outfield. Under the more common two- and three-umpire systems, a base umpire should leave the infield and move into the outfield if, *and only if,* a ball hit to the outfield is likely to result in a close play that will be hard for the plate umpire to call. This might include a sinking line drive that creates a possible trap situation or a ball hit near the outfield fence that could get lodged in the fence or that is difficult to judge as fair or foul. You will need to make this judgment very quickly after the ball is hit so you can move into the outfield fast enough to get a good view of the play.

If you need to cover a play in the outfield, you must communicate this by completely turning your back to the infield and hustling out to the play. You need to let the other umpires know that you have officially left the infield because doing so changes their responsibilities.

If you leave the infield for a ball hit to the outfield, you take all responsibility for the call—fair or foul, out or safe, live or dead. Once you have left the infield, *do not return* for the duration of the live action except to help in a rundown situation or to help with a play ahead. Never come back to a base where the initial call will be made.

Plays at the Bases

As a base umpire, you will get a lot of exercise moving around the field to get into position to make calls where most of the action happens—at the bases. Whether you are handling a routine out at first base, a sudden attempt to steal second or a rundown between second and third, you need to stay alert and tuned in to the game from start to finish. There are rules for special situations such as steals and rundowns, but regardless of what play action is occurring, the types of calls you will make most often on the bases are force plays and tag plays.

Force Plays

The principles behind calling a force play effectively are the same for each of the bases. Begin by moving into position as soon as the ball is hit. As the infielder is preparing to field the ground ball, move to the proper position. Depending on where the ball was hit, this should be approximately 15 to 18 feet from the base at a 90-degree angle to the path the thrown ball will travel. At its most basic, the decision point in this play is whether or not the fielder takes possession of the ball while touching the base prior to the runner touching the base. If the fielder does so, the runner is out. If not, the runner is safe.

Turn toward the base as the fielder releases the throw, and track the ball from the throwing fielder's hand to the fielder covering the base—let the ball take you into the play. When the throw is about halfway to its destination, move your eyes ahead of the ball to the receiving fielder's glove. This allows you to determine catch and control of the ball more quickly since you do not have to "find" it in the glove. At this time, focus on

- the base, to see if and when the runner touches it and
- the fielder, to see if and when the ball is officially caught.

Many things can happen to change the outcome at this critical point. The runner could miss the base, the fielder could miss or juggle the ball, or the runner and the fielder could even collide.

Be sure to maintain enough distance (15 to 18 feet) from the force play to be able to see the runner's point of contact with the base, the fielder's point of contact with the base and the fielder's glove catching the ball. Taking a position too close to the base restricts your viewing angle by narrowing your breadth of vision and may also cause you to get in the way of the play. This could result in the need to physically turn your head to look up at the glove of a reaching fielder, causing you to take your eyes off the base completely and thus preventing you from seeing when or if the runner touched the base.

The sound of the play can be helpful in determining the timing of the various components. While concentrating your vision primarily on the base and using your peripheral vision to watch the incoming ball and the fielder's glove, listen for the sound of the ball hitting the fielder's glove. Compare this moment to when you see the runner make contact with the base. Bear in mind that sound is an additional tool to help you make the right call, but vision will always be a more reliable means of determining whether the runner is out or safe. Noise from the crowd or the players could drown out the sound of the ball hitting the glove, or the ball may not hit the glove cleanly enough to create a sound.

Once you have gathered all the necessary information and the play is complete, hesitate slightly to form a mental picture of the play and to make it clear to all that you saw the play in its *entirety*. This hesitation should be barely perceptible but is important for ensuring you make the right call. In the past, this hesitation may have been considered a sign of indecision, but more modern umpiring theory has settled on the notion that this hesitation shows that you are more deliberate and in control.

As with nearly all calls, be very consistent with your timing and rhythm. If you are quick on some calls but use an exaggerated hesitation on others, it will appear to players and fans that you seem undecided. It is always better to be slow and correct than to be fast and wrong.

Once you have observed the play, have hesitated slightly and have made your decision, voice your call and show your signal as appropriate.

Tag Plays

Many of the elements discussed on force plays also apply to tag plays, such as position, angle and distance. The major difference is that on tag plays, you should be much closer to the play to be able to see whether the fielder's glove touches the runner. In some cases, this will be obvious, but in other cases, you will need to judge whether the very tip of the fielder's glove grazed the runner's jersey.

Start a normal distance from the play to keep all important elements within view. When the runner and ball begin converging where you believe a tag play might occur, move in quickly to within at least 10 to 12 feet at a 90-degree angle to the path of the runner (see figure 4.8).

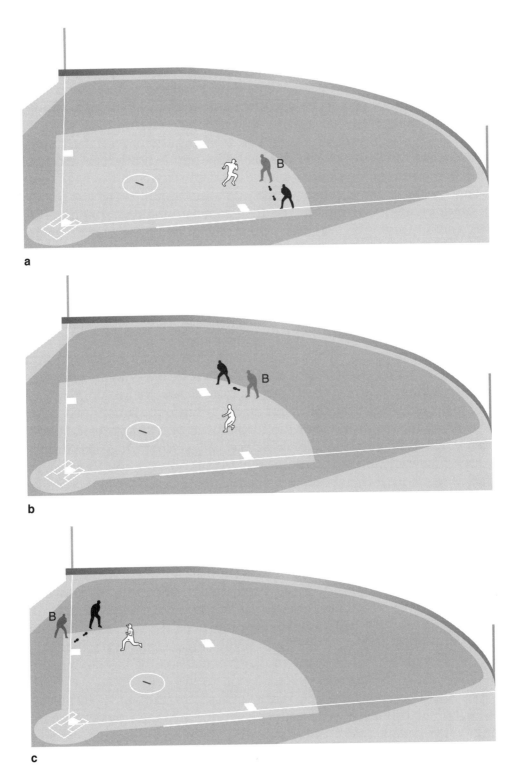

FIGURE 4.8 Calling a tag play at *(a)* first base, *(b)* second base and *(c)* third base.

The best viewing angle may change as the players move. When seeking an unobstructed angle, move with the play to avoid letting the defensive player or runner get between you and the tag. Keep the base in view if the tag play is near a base, especially if the runner is sliding.

Whether or not you are able to move into the ideal viewing position, when the moment of truth arrives, you need to concentrate on whether the tag was made prior to the runner reaching the base. If the runner makes it to the base prior to the tag being applied, the runner is safe unless the runner's motion continues and contact with the bag is lost while the tag is still applied.

Once the play is complete, use the proper timing and announce the call verbally and with a signal. A word of caution on tag plays: Contact between the runner and the fielder's glove can easily knock the ball out of the glove. Hesitation is *critical* on all tag plays to fully ensure that the fielder maintains possession of the ball long enough to warrant an out decision. Changing your call from out to safe after the ball falls out of the fielder's glove ranks in the top five most embarrassing umpire moments, so take your time and make the call only once!

If the tag happens close to what could have been a force-out at a base, point with your left hand and let everyone know the runner was out by calling, "Tag!" Verbally stating exactly *how* the runner was put out in order to "sell" the call is important because the runner may have looked quite safe in terms of the force-out. If you simply call, "Out!" many will think you have blown an easy call, since the tagout is harder to see. Generally, if the reason for making an out call (in this case, the tag) is the more difficult one to see, indicate the reason and then make the call.

If a hard slide causes a collision and you cannot find the ball after the tag is applied, tell the fielder in a firm voice, "Show me the ball." Point to the defensive player with your left hand while you are moving around the play trying to find the ball to indicate you are still focused on the play. Remain mobile as opposed to staying rooted in one position—move in and around the play if necessary to see the tag or to find the ball. Once you have found the ball, make the appropriate call. You need to be on top of this type of play quickly because the fielder could attempt to gain possession of the ball after the runner has reached the base to make it look as though the tag was made.

As with all plays, you should never "guess" a runner out. If you are not sure, call the runner safe or ask the plate umpire for assistance, explaining that you were obstructed from seeing the play. Or you may be able to call part of a play but need to ask for assistance on another part. For example, if you saw the catch beat the runner to first base but could not see whether the first-base player was on the base, you could ask the home plate umpire for assistance.

Ask what you need to know—in this case, "Did she have the bag?" If you ask for help on a particular aspect of a play, the call remains yours to make. Your partner should answer your question, after which you should make your ruling. If you ask for help with a call because you were blocked from seeing the play, you are transferring the call to your partner, who must then rule on the play. This should be a rare circumstance, however, as it is your job to see the play.

Should any confusion ensue, you can hold a quick, private huddle with your partner to sort it out. This is not recommended (and should not be necessary if the situation was covered in the pregame conference), because any time umpires must come together to talk, the perception of their game management abilities diminishes. However, sometimes it can prevent an uncertain situation from becoming a disaster. If you are missing information that you need to make a call, go get it.

Rundowns

A rundown occurs when a runner is trapped between bases (with no force in effect) and two or more defensive players attempt to tag the runner out. This is often an exciting action sequence that occurs suddenly, so you need to be prepared to adjust your field position for the best coverage of the rundown, depending on whether you are handling it yourself or with a crewmate.

If you are covering a rundown by yourself, move quickly to the best position to view both ends of the rundown where the final play might occur (the two bases on either side of the runner). The best position is about 12 feet away from the runner with a good view of both bases the runner might ultimately make a dash for. Move parallel to the base path the runner is on, maintaining your 12-foot distance (which may require you to slide back and forth between the bases a bit). You do not need to mirror the runner's entire movement back and forth—remember that the angle of view is always more important than your distance from the play. When the actual tag is attempted, move quickly into position to get the best angle on the play, then make your call with confidence.

If you have a crewmate to help you handle the rundown, each of you should take one end of the rundown to "bookend" the play. One umpire takes a position ahead of the runner and one behind the runner. Be sure to communicate with the other umpire by saying "I've got the lead!" or "I've got this end!" When possible, umpires should be on opposite sides of the runner's base path but should never cross the base path to establish this position.

A key point for handling rundowns is knowing who should make the call when the tag occurs. The rule is simple: The direction in which the runner is moving at the time of the tag dictates which umpire makes the call. In other words, if the runner is moving toward you, you make the call. If the runner is moving away from you, your partner makes the call.

Base Stealing in Fast Pitch

Base stealing is allowed in fast-pitch softball but not in slow pitch. When there is a runner on base, your preplay checklist should always include the possibility that the runner will steal, as well as an awareness of game situations that make an attempted steal more likely. When there is more than one runner on base, be sure to watch for a multiple-steal attempt. The suddenness of base stealing requires that you know your runner and base responsibilities clearly so no runner goes unmonitored after the action starts, as it may require a shifting of responsibilities.

Making and "Selling" the Call

Moving to the right position and knowing what to watch are key to being a good umpire, but the act of making—and, when necessary, "selling"—the call is every bit as important. Timing, presentation and emphasis all play a role in how your decision will be received by players, coaches and, of course, the fans, who *always* seem to think they have a better view than you do!

Previous sections covered situations where hesitation is proper before making a call. In determining how long to hesitate, be sure to watch other umpires to analyze their timing. Are they waiting long enough to have absolutely, positively, *definitely* seen the entire play? Or are they jumping the gun? Your hesitation should fall short of being theatrical but should be enough of a pause to communicate certainty.

Using the proper hand and arm signals, vocal calls and a combination of both as the game situation dictates takes practice but is extremely important. These signals are your means of communicating with players, coaches and fans and are your primary tools for maintaining control of the game. Your ability to tailor your style and emphasis to the game situation will develop quickly and will ultimately be one of your greatest assets for controlling the game. Although you may develop your own presentation style, you must always use the NFHS-approved signals as a standard means of communicating your calls.

Physical signals do not reinforce the verbal call. They *are* the call! Always keep in mind the players located farthest from you on the field (if not the farthest spectators) and make sure your signals are up, out and away from your body and are obvious enough to be seen by them. The signals must be distinct, deliberate, immediately understandable and held long enough to convey your conviction of the call. A quick note for lefties: On an overhand out, make the calls with the hand most comfortable for you—generally, the right hand for right-handed umpires and the left hand for left-handed umpires.

When the right moment arrives, *how* you actually make the call (physically and verbally) is important for demonstrating your competence and confidence, as well as for maintaining control of the game. If you communicate uncertainty through tentative calls, you may be in for a long day, with players on both sides questioning every call you make. Strike a balance between these two extremes and you will earn the respect and appreciation of the players and community you are serving.

Out and Safe Calls

You need to develop a range of emphasis for your physical and verbal signals to match the closeness of a call as well as its overall importance to the game. On the low end of the emphasis scale is the obvious play that even the players' parents would not argue about (for example, a throw to first that forces out a runner by 15 feet). You barely need to turn the intensity knob for such a routine play. Just calmly—but correctly, firmly and distinctly—offer up a simple "out" hand signal.

Routine Out Call

After getting into position to make the call, viewing the entire play and hesitating as appropriate, do the following:

1. From your slightly crouched position with your hands on your knees or thighs, keep your head forward and your eyes on the play, then rise to a standing position.
2. Bring your left hand in to your body, near your belt.
3. Give a brisk verbal call of "Out!" as your right arm forms a 90-degree hammer (see figure 4.9).

FIGURE 4.9   Making a routine out call.

Routine Safe Call

The procedure for making a routine safe call is similar:

1. From your slightly crouched position with your hands on your knees or thighs, keep your head forward and your eyes on the play, then rise to a standing position.

2. Bring both arms and hands—open with palms down—to your chest with the fingertips touching.

3. Give a brisk verbal call of "Safe!" while fully extending your arms outward so they are pointed sideways, away from your body and parallel to the ground, with the palms down (see figure 4.10).

FIGURE 4.10   Making a routine safe call.

A few notches up the intensity scale might be a tagout ending a rundown between second and third base. The tag was pretty obvious, but there was a lot of action leading up to the out. Match the excitement of the play with a flashier hand signal (perhaps with a little arm and body language) and a strong "Out!"

Even higher on the intensity scale might be a close tag play at third with the runner sliding into the base, just barely beating a throw from right field near the end of a close game. Hopes are high on both sides, so you need to "sell" the call to everyone in attendance with a forceful "Safe!" call accompanied by a powerful arm signal to let everyone know there is no question about the outcome (see figure 4.11).

FIGURE 4.11   Making a close safe call on a critical play.

Topping the charts might be a game-ending relay throw from second base resulting in a spectacular reaching tag by the catcher to barely tag a sliding runner for the out. A game-changing moment like this warrants a full overhand out signal accompanied by a convincing verbal call that emphasizes the importance of the play. The overhand out call begins the same as other calls, from the basic crouching stance. Watch the play from this position—hands on your knees or thighs, weight forward, knees slightly bent. After a slight hesitation to be certain the play is complete, rise to a standing position as you take a step with your left foot, moving directly at the play. Begin to raise your right arm above your head with your hand open. Shuffle your right foot, crossing it behind your left foot, much like a shortstop's feet might shuffle to make a strong throw to first base. Plant your right foot and push off with your left foot while stepping closer to the play as you bring your right arm over the top of your head in a throwing motion with a closed fist. Then give a vigorous "Out!" call as you drop the hammer (see figure 4.12).

Finish up by transferring your weight to your left foot while bringing your right foot forward and parallel to the left, about shoulder-width away, keeping your head in the play. You should conclude the throwing motion of your right arm by returning it to your knee. Remember, your movement should always take you closer to and directly at the play. When you finish "selling" the call, you'll be standing right on top of the play.

You get the idea—consider the closeness of the call as well as the importance of the play to the game. The closer the play or the more important it is to the game, the more emphasis you need to place on the call to make it very clear that you understand exactly what transpired and what is at stake. When you get near the high end of the emphasis scale, keep in mind a few important umpiring rules:

- Never make a call in a way that embarrasses or humiliates a player. Softball should help student-athletes grow as individuals in a competitive but supportive environment. Always keep your calls positive.

- The game is an opportunity for the players to excel and shine, not for you to make a bid for a highlight clip. If you want to entertain people, join your local theater group. On the field, your actions should facilitate the game, not divert attention from it.

FIGURE 4.12   *(a and b)* Making an overhand out call.

- Your behavior reflects on you as a professional, but also on the association of professional umpires you are part of. Do your part to uphold the high standards of professionalism expected of umpires.

Different situations call for you to display a variety of call styles to suit the play. Following are a few special notes on "selling" calls that will help you perform like a pro:

- If you must rule a runner out as a result of an appeal, a simple overhand out call will suffice.

- Attempted steals (fast pitch), close force plays, most rundowns and almost all tag plays are generally close plays that require greater call intensity.

Ten Keys for Successful Base Umpiring

1. Always keep all four elements of a play in view—the ball, the runner, the base and the fielder. If you follow your positioning guidelines, you will almost always be in a good position to judge a play.

2. Move parallel with the runner when moving into position for a call.

3. Hustle! You will be in a better position to view plays and make calls if you keep on the move, and you will also be less likely to draw the ire of players or fans if you are clearly working hard.

4. Get ready to move on all pitched, batted and thrown balls—you never know when you'll need that extra second to get on top of a play, so stay on your toes!

5. Wait for a play to be *truly and finally complete* before you make a call (except in the case of delayed dead-ball or dead-ball calls where you need to signal *immediately*). Avoid making two calls on a play.

6. You are the umpire, and your responsibilities are yours alone. Do not let players or coaches call plays for you or even get on your nerves. Their satisfaction with the outcome of the game is not your concern.

7. Adjust your calls and signals to the obviousness and importance of a play. Save your forceful calls for big plays and use routine signals for routine plays. Only make calls when necessary—for example, a safe call is not necessary on an errant throw that gets by the first-base player. No ball, no call.

8. Line up runners on all fly balls to the outfield so you can clearly view the timing of their departure from the base(s) relative to the moment a catch is made. Be sure to position yourself so that you are out of the way of the players. Make sure you have a clear view and that you are not obstructing any defensive player's view.

9. Hustle into the outfield on fly balls that will be difficult for the plate umpire to call.

10. Once you leave the infield, stay out for the duration of the play, unless you need to come back in for help with a rundown or help ahead, never on the initial play at a base.

- On attempts to pick runners off base (fast pitch), a routine signal may be given unless the play is close, in which case you should "sell" the call a bit.
- Be aware that play may continue after your call. Stay out of the way of the players and get ready for your next call.

With practice, you will develop a range of emphasis for all your calls. The best approach is to start easy by setting a baseline for routine calls and building in intensity as necessary. Be sure to leave some extra intensity in reserve—do not give everything you have on the first few plays of the game because you will have nowhere to go.

Occasionally you will need to make a call based on a particular aspect of the play that will not be obvious to anyone; in fact, it may have been apparent *only* to you. For example, consider a force play at first where the first-base fielder's foot is pulled before the ball is caught, making the runner who appears to be out actually safe. In such situations, use the true reason for your decision to "sell" the call before you make it. In this example, do so by pointing at the bag and stating the reason, using "foot" or a similar word that gets the point across, and then announce your call (safe, in this example). You should only use this extra explanation (and any hand gestures—generally pointing) when the less obvious of two factors caused the call. This will help you avoid controversy by making clear why the call was made. Players may disagree with the reason you are *not* citing for the call (the actual timing of the force-out in the case described above), but they will understand better and be less likely to argue if you articulate why the call was made.

CHAPTER 5

One-, Two- and Three-Umpire Mechanics

Two- and three-umpire systems are used most commonly in high school softball today, although one- and occasionally even four-umpire systems are used as well. The system used generally depends on regional regulations, finances available and population density, with more umpires used for higher, more competitive high school divisions.

The two-umpire system is the most popular because it provides good field coverage (considerably better than a single umpire can provide) yet does not require league administrators to find and hire three or more umpires for every game. Although the four-umpire system provides complete field coverage and is sometimes used for important playoffs or tournaments, the two- and three-umpire systems are generally considered more than adequate. Because the four-umpire system is seldom used, it is not covered in this chapter.

One-Umpire System

The one-umpire system is still used in some areas of the country, but only in slow pitch, and is generally not a recommended umpiring solution. However, you could end up umpiring a game alone due to logistical problems that prevent other umpires from attending, so you should know how to handle a game by yourself in case the need arises. Because play coverage with the one-umpire system is not adequate to make good calls at all locations on the field, it should only be used when necessary.

The good news about the one-umpire system is that the mechanics are simple to learn. Since there is no one to share responsibilities with, there is no question about who is covering what plays—you are covering everything. The bad news is it's not easy to umpire an entire game by yourself.

With a single umpire, the recommended starting position before every pitch is behind home plate. From this vantage point you can

- call balls and strikes and cover home plate,
- view the entire field and see plays as they are developing,
- move quickly into the infield to cover bases as necessary and
- rule fair or foul on balls hit down the lines.

Coverage Strategies

Umpiring solo takes a tremendous amount of hustle, alertness and keen anticipation to make sure you get a view of every play. The main challenge when working alone is that you can only watch one play at a time. If you are focused on a play at third, how will you know if the batter-runner touched first base before heading to second? You probably won't in some situations. There is no good solution for this limitation of the system, which is why the two- and three-umpire systems are strongly preferred. The rule discussed earlier—do not "guess" a player out—applies here as well. If you could not see the play and have no concrete reason to believe the runner should be called out, the runner should be considered safe.

On each batted ball, move out from behind the plate and into the infield to obtain the best position for any play that develops. Recall from your positioning training (see chapter 4) that getting a good angle of view is more important than your distance from the play. Your ability to anticipate where plays will occur is more important than ever. For example, watch the feet of an outfielder making a throw to know which infielder will receive the ball, then move quickly to position yourself where the play will occur. Fielders will step toward their intended throwing target, giving you some advance notice where the ball is headed.

Keeping your eye on the ball is vital when umpiring alone because there are no other umpires to keep track of it and back you up. Sometimes this is impossible because plays develop so quickly and errors occur, sending the ball out of your field of view. For example, a very challenging play would be calling a third out at third base when a runner is attempting to score at home. You need to verify the out at third, then turn your attention to home plate to see whether the out was made before the runner crossed the plate. Once the runner has scored, you must turn back to third base to verify that the fielder held onto the ball. Clearly, this system is not as effective as having one umpire calling the play at third and another watching the timing of the runner crossing the plate. However, if done properly you can still make the call with confidence. As long as you concentrate on looking in the right place at the right time and turn quickly, you can handle this and other difficult timing plays.

Try to position yourself as close as possible to all play situations, especially tag plays that require a closer view. Keep in mind that a defensive play cannot happen without the ball, so your first priority is always the location of the ball. Cover the play where the ball is located, then quickly turn to any other action on the diamond.

Field Positioning

With no runners on base, make all calls from inside the diamond. This allows you to cover any of the bases with minimal chance of causing obstruction by pivoting.

If there is a play at home, position yourself at the left rear of the right-hand batter's box (see figure 5.1). This position should ensure a good angle for viewing any play at home plate (the ball, the runner and the catcher) and it also preserves your view of the rest of the field so you can verify that runners are tagging bases.

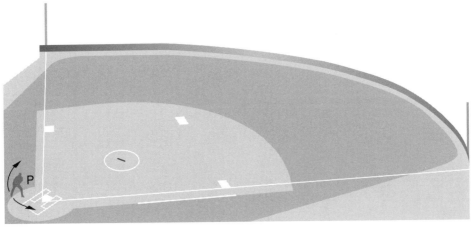

FIGURE 5.1   One-umpire positioning for calling a play at home.

When you need to cover first, second or third base, use your judgment based on the overall runner situation. If the bases are loaded and the ball is hit, you do not want to run all the way out to second base because you will be out of position to see home plate and third base, where plays are likely to occur. Keep the number of outs and the score in mind in anticipating the defensive team's actions. Do they need to prevent a run? If so, they are likely to make a play at home plate. If there are two outs, they will likely attempt to make an out at the easiest base, depending on where the ball is hit. Think through the game situation before each pitch, and do your best to anticipate the location of the action, but be prepared to pivot quickly to make a call anywhere.

Once all play has ceased, you may call a time-out while you return to your position behind home plate.

The keys to successfully umpiring a game on your own are hustling and positioning. On every play, you need to get out from behind the plate quickly and move a short distance into the infield (staying out of players' way), and always be ready to pivot and move into a play to get a good view. You will often need to make more than one call in sequence, so stay focused until all play is over.

Recommended movement and positioning for a single umpire are shown below. Compare the items in each list to the movement pattern shown in the illustration.

No Runners on Base

In all of the following base-hit situations, the umpire in a one-umpire system must watch the runner tag bases and be aware of the position of the ball when there are no runners on base (see figure 5.2).

- A: No runners—single
- B: No runners—double
- C: No runners—triple
- D: No runners—home run

FIGURE 5.2   One-umpire positioning for no runners on base.

Ground Balls to Infield

In all of the following ground-ball situations, the umpire in a one-umpire system must watch the runner tag bases and be aware of the position of the ball when there are no runners on base (see figure 5.3).

- A: Ground ball—no runners on
- B: Ground ball—runner on first base or runners on first and second
- C: Ground ball—runner on third base, runners on second and third, first and third, or bases loaded

FIGURE 5.3   One-umpire positioning for ground balls to the infield.

Fly-Ball Situation

In all fly-ball situations where the ball is near the foul line, the umpire, in a one-umpire system, must stay on the foul line to determine whether the ball is fair or foul, then move into the infield to pick up runners and plays (see figure 5.4).

- A: No runners—fly ball to infield or outfield and not near the foul line
- B: Runner on first base
- C: Runners on first and second or second only—move to a possible call at third or into foul territory ahead of the lead runner for a possible play at home after the catch
- D: Runners on second and third or first and third

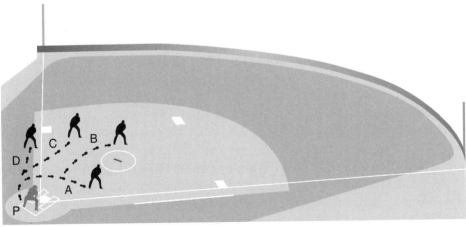

FIGURE 5.4   One-umpire positioning for fly-ball situations.

Between-Inning Mechanics

Assume a position approximately 20 feet from home plate, near the line in foul territory and facing the infield. Alternate foul lines by taking a position on the foul line that is on the side of the team that is taking the field to play defense. This will give you a good view of the on-deck circle and the dugout of the team coming to bat (see figure 5.5).

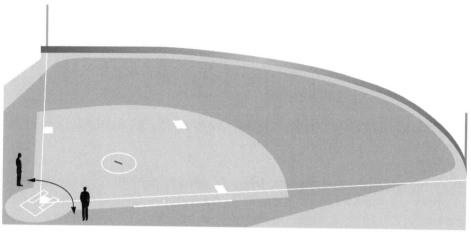

FIGURE 5.5   One-umpire positioning between innings.

Two-Umpire System

The two-umpire system is very effective for covering all plays that occur on the field in both fast- and slow-pitch softball. A few differences in coverage between the two styles of softball are detailed toward the end of the two-umpire section.

Under the two-umpire system, there is a plate umpire and a single base umpire. The plate umpire (shown as P in diagrams) has all the standard plate umpire responsibilities, including balls and strikes, plays at the plate, managing the timing of the game and everything else discussed in chapter 3. The base umpire (shown as B in the following diagrams) is primarily responsible for the bases, some plays in the outfield and for monitoring special rules such as pitching violations and helping with checked swings.

The same infield/outfield responsibility mechanics apply if the base umpire moves into the outfield to make a call (anticipating a trap, two players converging on the ball or a ball near the outfield fence). In this case, the plate umpire assumes complete responsibility for the infield, including all runners and bases—essentially, the infield reverts to a one-umpire system with the plate umpire working alone.

Several specific situations where responsibilities change based on the game situation are covered in detail in the following pages. However, the basic responsibilities remain the same:

- In all situations, the plate umpire calls fair or foul on all batted balls near the foul lines. The plate umpire must move up the foul line to make these calls, remembering not to make the call too early.
- The plate umpire must always be ready to assist with rundowns but must not abandon home plate to do so if a play is likely to occur there. For example, if there is a runner on third and a rundown develops between first and second, you will not be able to help with the rundown, as you must be ready for a play at the plate or third base.
- On routine fly balls to the outfield, the plate umpire (with no runners on or a runner at first base) would go to the center of the infield in the direction of the batted ball to make the catch/no-catch call. With runners in scoring position, the plate umpire must stay in foul territory near home plate to be ready for a possible play at the plate. With runners on base, the base umpire should move inside the bases to watch the assigned runner tag-ups.
- In fast-pitch softball, the base umpire must be ready for snap throws by the catcher and possible pickoff attempts by the pitcher on the base runners.
- Both umpires must hustle at all times and never take their eyes off the ball.
- The key to success with the two-umpire system is to communicate with your partner, since responsibilities sometimes overlap—remember, if you deviate, communicate!

Base Responsibilities

The plate umpire has additional responsibilities for plays on the bases under the two-umpire system. In addition to having responsibility for all plays at home, including seeing the runner touch the plate, the plate umpire is responsible for any play (except the first play in the infield by an infielder) and for seeing the lead runner touch third.

To cover the lead runner, the plate umpire must first move to a "holding zone" in foul territory between home and third base. The plate umpire then picks up the lead runner and prepares to make any necessary call at either third base or home plate. In some situations, the base umpire will take responsibility for third base (to be discussed shortly), but the home plate umpire always calls all plays at home plate.

If there are two runners on and the next batter hits for extra bases, which will likely score the lead runner without a play, as plate umpire, you would pay little attention to the scoring runner other than noting whether third base and the plate were touched. You would then direct your attention to the second runner and any play that may be made. Meanwhile, the base umpire must ascertain whether all runners touch first and second bases and is responsible for any play made on the batter-runner. If the batter-runner advances past second base and a play is made at third, it is the base umpire's responsibility. If it is the third out of the inning, the base umpire should quickly and vociferously make the call so the plate umpire can announce whether a runner scoring on the same play has touched home before the third out was made (a timing play).

The base umpire is responsible for the call at third base in the following five situations:

1. The batter-runner or any single runner (runner on first tagging and advancing on a caught fly ball) who advances to third.

2. Any trail runners that attempt to reach third base. In this case, the plate umpire is responsible for the lead runner and thus is not available to make calls at third.

3. Any return throw from the catcher or other player who has cut off a throw to home plate. This situation would indicate a possible play at home plate, and thus the plate umpire is focused there, requiring the base umpire to take responsibility for third base.

4. A throw by the catcher immediately following the pitch (fast pitch) in an attempt to pick off a runner occupying third base or to put out a runner stealing third. In this case, the plate umpire is focused on the pitch and any possible action created by the batter, requiring the base umpire to take responsibility for a quick call at third base.

5. The first play in the infield by an infielder.

Runner Violations

In fast pitch, a runner may legally leave her base and attempt to advance to another base when the ball leaves the pitcher's hand on delivery of the pitch. In slow pitch, a runner cannot leave the base until the batter makes contact with the pitch, the ball touches the ground or reaches home plate.

Both the plate and the base umpire have equal authority to call a runner out for leaving a base too soon (the timing requirements differ for fast- and slow-pitch softball).

In fast pitch, the umpire should observe the runner's foot on the base and peripherally watch the arm swing of the pitcher. Once the pitcher's arm is in a straight line with the body, the pitch is considered to be released. In slow pitch, the base umpire should observe the batter out of the corner of her eye to know when the moment the runner is legally able to advance arrives. The plate umpire must always be focused on the pitcher, the pitch and home plate. Although the plate umpire can see the runners peripherally, he or she probably cannot make as accurate a timing determination as the base umpire, especially if properly focused on the incoming pitch. Thus, even though the plate umpire can make this call, it is better left to the base umpire, who can devote full concentration to that play. As with other plays, do not "guess" a runner out—be sure the runner actually left the base too soon before enforcing a penalty.

Fly-Ball Tag Responsibilities
In both fast and slow pitch, the plate and base umpires have responsibilities during a tag. These tag-up procedures should be followed at all times unless there is communication between umpires to modify them.

The plate umpire has the following tag responsibilities:

- All runners at third base
- The runner at second base with runners at first and second

The base umpire has the following tag responsibilities:

- All runners at first base
- All runners at second base only
- The runner at second base with runners at second and third
- Runners at first and second base when the bases are loaded

Positioning

The starting position for the plate umpire in the two-umpire system is always behind home plate. The base umpire has three different starting positions, depending on where runners are located. These are positions A, B and C and will be covered later in the chapter.

In this section, we'll cover all the situations you will face in a two-umpire crew:

- No runners on base
- Runner on first
- Runner on second
- Runner on third
- Runners on first and second
- Runners on second and third
- Runners on first and third
- Bases loaded

For each situation, we'll provide the mechanics and coverage for the plate umpire and the base umpire.

No Runners on Base

The starting position for the plate umpire when there are no runners on base is standard—directly behind home plate, ready to watch the pitch. This is the simplest of the base runner scenarios because you only need to keep track of the batter-runner in the event of a hit.

As the base umpire, with no runners on base, you should be 15 to 18 feet beyond the base, completely in foul territory (position A in figure 5.2, on page 78). You are also responsible for the batter-runner all the way to third base.

Hits to the Infield

When there are no runners on base, both the plate and base umpires have specific areas of coverage and positions on a hit to the infield. See figure 5.6 for these areas and positions.

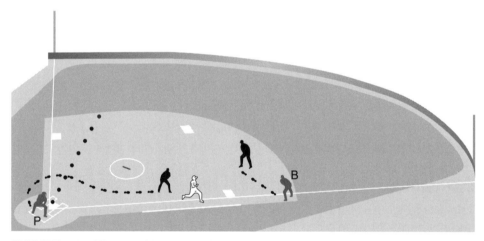

FIGURE 5.6   Plate and base umpire responsibilities for hits to the infield with no runners on base.

- *Plate umpire.* If a ball is hit close to a line, move to the line and make any fair/foul call on the ball. Stay behind the ball and trail the batter-runner to first base. You are responsible for the ball if overthrown and for the batter-runner at home plate.
- *Base umpire.* From position A, move into fair territory, staying on the outfield side of the diamond, and make any call at first base. You are responsible for the batter-runner at first, second and third.

Hits to the Outfield

When there are no runners on base, both the plate and base umpires have specific areas of coverage and positions on a hit to the outfield. See figure 5.7 for these areas and positions.

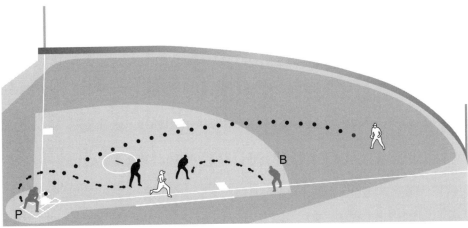

FIGURE 5.7   Plate and base umpire responsibilities for hits to the outfield with no runners on base.

- *Plate umpire.* If a ball is hit close to a line, move to the line and make any fair/foul call on the ball. Otherwise, move out from behind the plate toward the pitching circle. Be prepared to assist in a rundown. You are responsible for the batter-runner at home plate.
- *Base umpire.* Pivot inside the diamond in fair territory. You are responsible for the batter-runner at first, second and third.

Fly Balls

When there are no runners on base, both the plate and base umpires have specific areas of coverage and positions for fly balls. See figure 5.8 for these areas and positions.

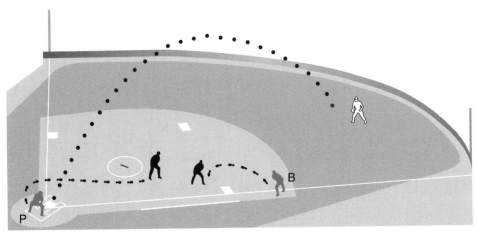

FIGURE 5.8   Plate and base umpire responsibilities for fly balls to the outfield with no runners on base.

- *Plate umpire.* For fly balls that are not close to a foul line, move to the center of the infield in the direction of the batted ball. The plate umpire, on ground balls hit close to the foul line, should stay at home plate on the line and make the call. The plate umpire, on infield hits, moves up the first-base line, observing the play, and is prepared to help his partner.
- *Base umpire.* If hit to the outfield, pivot inside the diamond at first base. If hit to the infield, move into fair territory, staying outside the diamond. You are responsible for the batter-runner at first, second and third.

Runner on First

The starting position for the plate umpire with a runner on first base is standard—directly behind home plate, ready to watch the pitch (see figure 5.9).

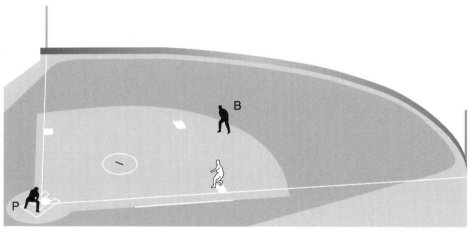

FIGURE 5.9 Starting positions for plate and base umpires with a runner on first base.

As the base umpire, your starting position is about 20 feet from first base toward second base and outside the baseline. This position will normally place you two or three steps behind and to the left of the second-base player.

Hits to the Infield

When there is a runner on first base, both the plate and base umpires have specific areas of coverage and positions on a hit to the infield. See figure 5.10 for these areas and positions.

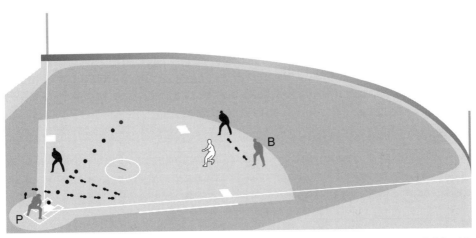

FIGURE 5.10 Plate and base umpire responsibilities for hits to the infield with a runner on first base.

- *Plate umpire.* On batted balls to the infield, leave to the left of the catcher, moving up the first-base line to observe the play, then fade toward third base to cover the advancing runner.
- *Base umpire.* From your starting position, watch the fielder field the ball and let the throw take you to the play at either second or first base. You are responsible for all plays at first and second and for the batter-runner all the way to third base.

Hits to the Outfield

When there is a runner on first base, both the plate and base umpires have specific areas of coverage and positions on a hit to the outfield. See figure 5.11 for these areas and positions.

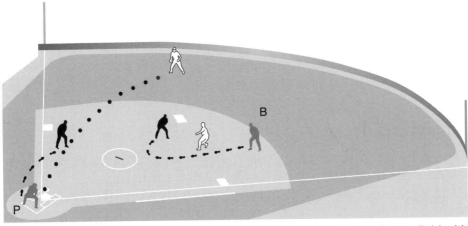

FIGURE 5.11 Plate and base umpire responsibilities for hits to the outfield with a runner on first base.

- *Plate umpire.* Move toward third base to handle any play that develops, but be prepared to drop back toward home plate to make any calls at home.
- *Base umpire.* On base hits to the outfield, immediately come inside the diamond, buttonhook, take any play at first and second and take the batter-runner all the way to third base.

Fly Balls

When there is a runner on first base, both the plate and base umpires have specific areas of coverage and positions for fly balls. See figure 5.12 for these areas and positions.

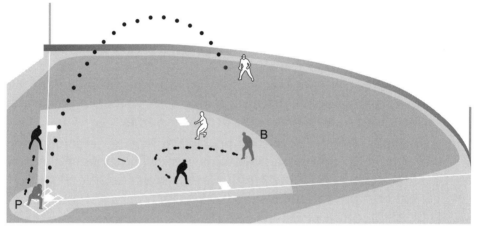

FIGURE 5.12   Plate and base umpire responsibilities for fly balls with a runner on first base.

- *Plate umpire.* For fly balls that are not close to a foul line, move to the center of the infield in the direction of the batted ball. Be prepared to move to third base if the lead runner advances beyond second base.
- *Base umpire.* If a fly ball is hit to the outfield, you are responsible for the tag-up at first base and for that runner all the way to third base.

Runner on Second

The starting position for the plate umpire with a runner on second base is directly behind home plate, ready to call the pitch.

As the base umpire, your starting position is a few steps behind and to the left of the shortstop. Take care not to interfere with the outfielder's view of the batter or an infield play (see figure 5.13).

FIGURE 5.13   Starting positions for plate and base umpires with a runner on second base.

Hits to the Infield

When there is a runner on second base, both the plate and base umpires have specific areas of coverage and positions on a hit to the infield. See figure 5.14 for these areas and positions.

FIGURE 5.14   Plate and base umpire responsibilities for hits to the infield with a runner on second base.

- *Plate umpire.* On batted balls to the infield, you are responsible for any plays at third base. Use the first-base line extended to fulfill your trail responsibilities if the play goes to first. Be prepared to move quickly to third for a subsequent play at third base and to move quickly back to home plate if the runner advances beyond third.

- *Base umpire.* You are also responsible for all plays at first and second and the batter-runner at third.

Hits to the Outfield

When there is a runner on second base, both the plate and base umpires have specific areas of coverage and positions on a hit to the outfield. See figure 5.15 for these areas and positions.

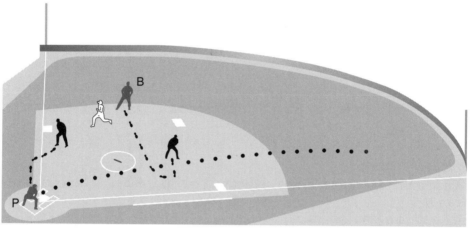

FIGURE 5.15   Plate and base umpire responsibilities for hits to the outfield with a runner on second base.

- *Plate umpire.* Move down the left-field foul line in foul territory toward third base. See the runner touch third and take any play at third or home on the lead runner.
- *Base umpire.* On base hits to the outfield, immediately come inside the diamond, buttonhook and take the batter-runner all the way to third base.

Fly Balls

When there is a runner on second base, both the plate and base umpires have specific areas of coverage and positions for fly balls. See figure 5.16 for these areas and positions.

- *Plate umpire.* Move from behind home plate toward third base. Be prepared to move into the infield for the play at third on the advancing runner or back to home plate (if the runner continues past third).
- *Base umpire.* Move into the infield between the pitching plate and the baseline. You are responsible for the tag-up of the runner at second base.

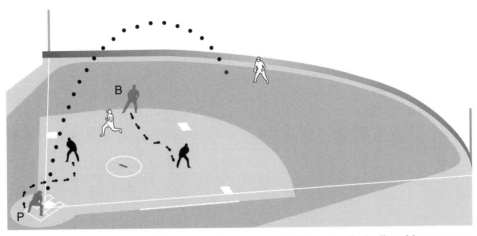

FIGURE 5.16   Plate and base umpire responsibilities for fly balls with a runner on second base.

Runner on Third

The starting position for the plate umpire with a runner on third base is directly behind home plate, ready to call the pitch. The main consideration in this scenario is a likely play at the plate.

As the base umpire, your starting position is a few steps behind and to the right of the shortstop (see figure 5.17). Take care not to interfere with the outfielder's view of the batter or an infield play.

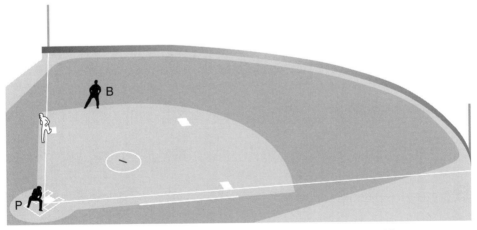

FIGURE 5.17   Starting positions for plate and base umpires with a runner on third base.

Hits to the Infield

When there is a runner on third base, both the plate and base umpires have specific areas of coverage and positions on a hit to the infield. See figure 5.18 for these areas and positions.

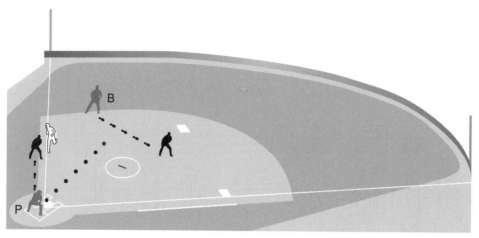

FIGURE 5.18   Plate and base umpire responsibilities for hits to the infield with a runner on third base.

- *Plate umpire.* On batted balls to the infield, you are responsible for any play at home plate and subsequent play at third base.
- *Base umpire.* You are responsible for any play that develops from the first throw unless the throw is to home plate. Wait for the fielder to commit, then move quickly toward the base where the ball is being thrown.

Hits to the Outfield
When there is a runner on third base, both the plate and base umpires have specific areas of coverage and positions on a hit to the outfield. See figure 5.19 for these areas and positions.

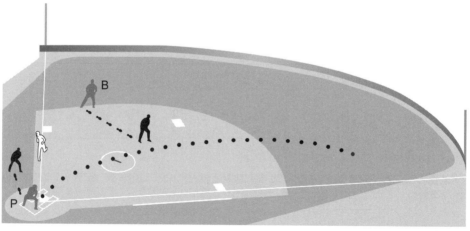

FIGURE 5.19   Plate and base umpire responsibilities for hits to the outfield with a runner on third base.

- *Plate umpire.* Watch the runner touch home or take the play at home.
- *Base umpire.* Immediately come inside the diamond toward first base. Take the batter-runner all the way to third base.

Fly Balls

When there is a runner on third base, both the plate and base umpires have specific areas of coverage and positions for fly balls. See figure 5.20 for these areas and positions.

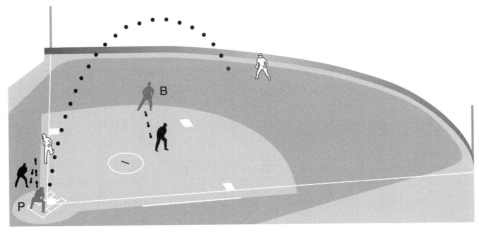

FIGURE 5.20   Plate and base umpire responsibilities for fly balls with a runner on third base.

- *Plate umpire.* Move between home plate and third base in foul territory. Watch the runner tag up at third. Be prepared to take the play at third or to move back to home plate quickly if the runner attempts to score.
- *Base umpire.* Be prepared to follow the batter-runner if the catch is not made.

Runners on First and Second

The starting position for the plate umpire with runners on first and second is—you guessed it—behind home plate, ready to call the pitch.

As the base umpire, your starting position is a few steps behind and to the left of the shortstop (see figure 5.21).

Hits to the Infield

When there are runners on first and second base, both the plate and base umpires have specific areas of coverage and positions on a hit to the infield. See figure 5.22 for these areas and positions.

FIGURE 5.21 Starting positions for plate and base umpires with runners on first and second base.

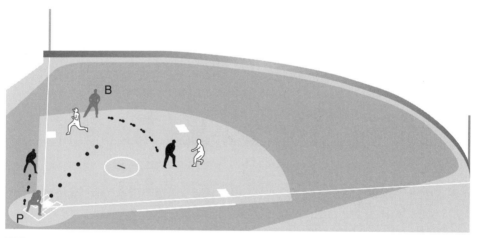

FIGURE 5.22 Plate and base umpire responsibilities for hits to the infield with runners on first and second base.

- *Plate umpire.* If the play goes to first, start drifting toward third while watching for your trail responsibilities at first. Take any subsequent play at third and any play at home. Move toward third base to make a call on any play, and be ready to return to home plate quickly if the runner advances past third.
- *Base umpire.* Take the first throw unless it is to home plate. If the first throw is to first, second or third base, the plate umpire covers any subsequent throw to third base.

Hits to the Outfield

When there are runners on first and second base, both the plate and base umpires have specific areas of coverage and positions on a hit to the outfield. See figure 5.23 for these areas and positions.

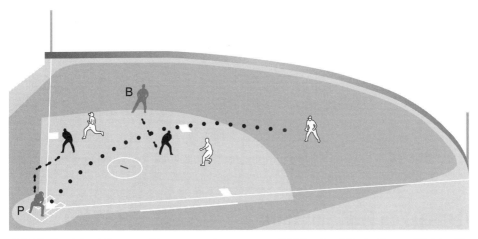

FIGURE 5.23   Plate and base umpire responsibilities for hits to the outfield with runners on first and second base.

- *Plate umpire.* You are responsible for taking the lead runner into third base and to home. Be prepared to make a call at third base by moving down the line toward third when the ball is hit. Once you are within 15 feet of the base, move into the infield for a good angle on the play at third. You are responsible for any play at the plate as well, so be ready to move quickly back toward home.
- *Base umpire.* On base hits to the outfield, you are responsible for any play at second base and for taking the batter-runner all the way to third base. Move inside the diamond, buttonhook and be prepared for a play at second.

Fly Balls

When there are runners on first and second base, both the plate and base umpires have specific areas of coverage and positions for fly balls. See figure 5.24 for these areas and positions.

- *Plate umpire.* Move from behind home plate toward second base to get a good view of the outfielder attempting the catch and the lead runner at second base—you are responsible for the tag-up at second and any play on this runner at second, third or home.
- *Base umpire.* You are responsible for the tag-up of the runner at first base. Move quickly inside the diamond directly toward first base. Be prepared to take this runner to second.

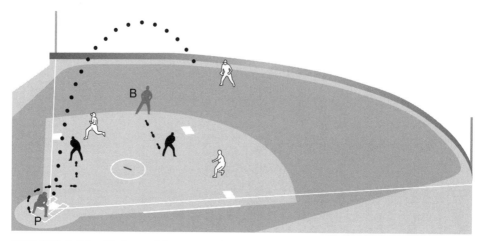

FIGURE 5.24   Plate and base umpire responsibilities for fly balls with runners on first and second base.

Runners on First and Third

The starting position for the plate umpire with runners on first and third base is directly behind home plate, ready to call the pitch. The main consideration in this scenario is a likely play at the plate.

As the base umpire, your starting position is a few steps behind and to the right of the shortstop (see figure 5.25). Take care not to interfere with the outfielder's view of the batter or an infield play.

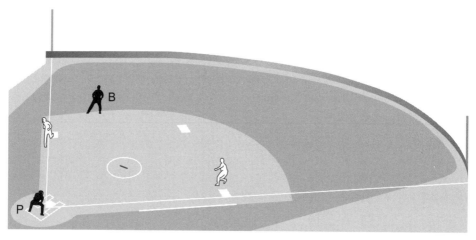

FIGURE 5.25   Starting positions for plate and base umpires with runners on first and third base.

Hits to the Infield

When there are runners on first and third base, both the plate and base umpires have specific areas of coverage and positions on a hit to the infield. See figure 5.26 for these areas and positions.

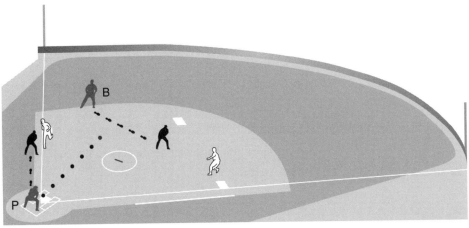

FIGURE 5.26 Plate and base umpire responsibilities for hits to the infield with runners on first and third base.

- *Plate umpire.* On batted balls to the infield, you are responsible for any play at home plate and subsequent play at third base.
- *Base umpire.* You are responsible for any play that develops from the first throw unless the throw is to home plate. Wait for the fielder to commit, then move quickly toward the base where the ball is being thrown.

Hits to the Outfield

When there are runners on first and third base, both the plate and base umpires have specific areas of coverage and positions on a hit to the outfield. See figure 5.27 for these areas and positions.

- *Plate umpire.* Watch the runner touch home or take the play at home and drift back to the holding zone at third for a possible play there.
- *Base umpire.* On base hits to the outfield, you are responsible for any play at second base and for taking the batter-runner all the way to third base. Move inside the diamond, buttonhook and be prepared for a play at second.

Fly Balls

When there are runners on first and third base, both the plate and base umpires have specific areas of coverage and positions for fly balls. See figure 5.28 for these areas and positions.

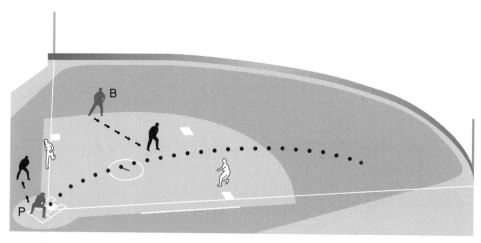

FIGURE 5.27 Plate and base umpire responsibilities for hits to the outfield with runners on first and third base.

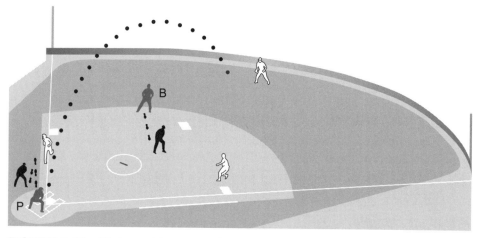

FIGURE 5.28 Plate and base umpire responsibilities for fly balls with runners on first and third base.

- *Plate umpire.* Move between home plate and third base in foul territory. Watch the runner tag up at third. Be prepared to take the play at third or to move back to home plate quickly if the runner attempts to score.

- *Base umpire.* You are responsible for the tag-up of the runner at first base. Move quickly inside the diamond directly toward first base. Be prepared to take this runner to second.

Runners on Second and Third

As with any time there are runners in scoring position (second or third), you, as the plate umpire, must be ready to cover plays at the plate. The team at bat is trying to score, after all!

As the base umpire, your starting position is a few steps behind and to the right of the shortstop (see figure 5.29).

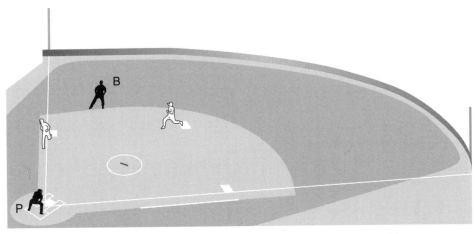

FIGURE 5.29   Starting positions for plate and base umpires with runners on second and third base.

Hits to the Infield

When there are runners on second and third base, both the plate and base umpires have specific areas of coverage and positions on a hit to the infield. See figure 5.30 for these areas and positions.

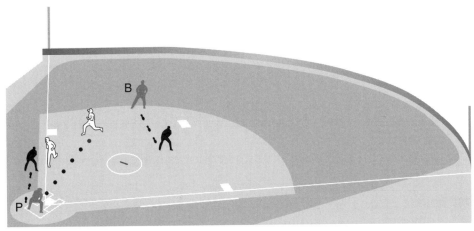

FIGURE 5.30   Plate and base umpire responsibilities for hits to the infield with runners on second and third base.

- *Plate umpire.* If a play is made at first base, hang back at the plate for your trail duties. Be prepared for a subsequent play at third or home on the lead runner. If the lead runner scores, turn your attention and move toward third base to call any plays there.
- *Base umpire.* Take the first throw unless it is to home plate. If the first throw is to first, second or third base, the plate umpire covers any subsequent throw to third base on the lead runner.

Hits to the Outfield

When there are runners on second and third base, both the plate and base umpires have specific areas of coverage and positions on a hit to the outfield. See figure 5.31 for these areas and positions.

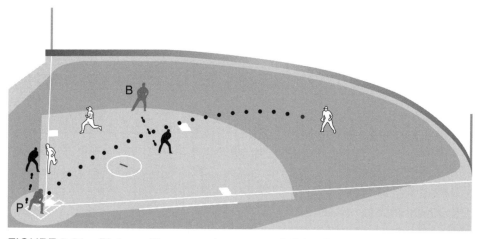

FIGURE 5.31   Plate and base umpire responsibilities for hits to the outfield with runners on second and third base.

- *Plate umpire.* Move toward third base. If the lead runner advances home and there will be no play, continue to drift toward third, preparing for a play there. Watch the lead runner touch home plate as you do so. If there is a play at home, move quickly to a position toward the left rear of the right-hand batter's box to make the call.
- *Base umpire.* On base hits to the outfield that you do not follow into the outfield, move inside the diamond and take the batter-runner all the way to third base, as needed. Be prepared to take the runner from second into third if the lead runner has not scored or is just scoring on a play at the plate.

Fly Balls

When there are runners on second and third base, both the plate and base umpires have specific areas of coverage and positions for fly balls. See figure 5.32 for these areas and positions.

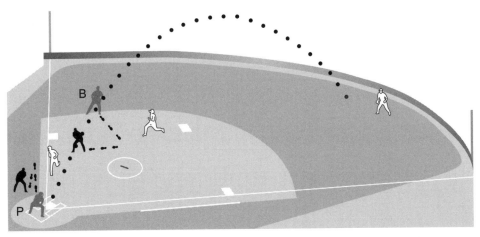

FIGURE 5.32 Plate and base umpire responsibilities for fly balls with runners on second and third base.

- *Plate umpire.* Move from behind home plate to get a good view of the outfielder attempting the catch and the lead runner at third base—you are responsible for the tag-up at third. Be prepared for a play at the plate.
- *Base umpire.* Move into the infield quickly, turn and line up the runner on second base to call the tag-up, and follow that runner to third base, as needed.

Bases Loaded

Runners at first, second and third—a major scoring opportunity for the batting team! The plate umpire needs to be ready to cover any plays at the plate. As the base umpire, your starting position is a few steps behind and to the right of the shortstop (see figure 5.33).

Hits to the Infield

When the bases are loaded, both the plate and base umpires have specific areas of coverage and positions on a hit to the infield. See figure 5.34 for these areas and positions.

- *Plate umpire.* If a play is made at first base, watch your trail responsibilities while seeing the lead runner touch home plate, then move toward third base to call any plays there.
- *Base umpire.* Take the first throw unless it is to home plate. If the first throw is to first, second or third base, the plate umpire covers any subsequent throw to third base.

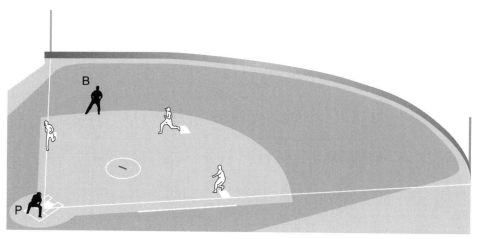

FIGURE 5.33   Starting positions for plate and base umpires with the bases loaded.

FIGURE 5.34   Plate and base umpire responsibilities for hits to the infield with the bases loaded.

Hits to the Outfield

When the bases are loaded, both the plate and base umpires have specific areas of coverage and positions on a hit to the outfield. See figure 5.35 for these areas and positions.

- *Plate umpire.* Move toward third base in foul territory. If the lead runner advances home and there will be no play, continue to drift toward third, preparing for a play there. Watch the lead runner touch home plate as you do so. If there is a play at home, move quickly to a position toward the left rear of the right-hand batter's box to make the call at home.

- *Base umpire.* On base hits to the outfield that you do not follow into the outfield, move inside the diamond and be prepared to make a call at first, second or third base.

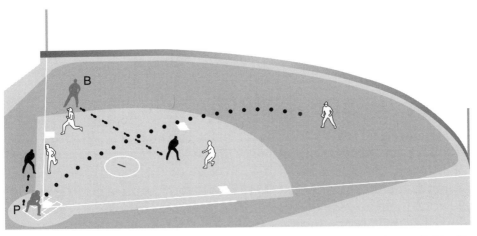

FIGURE 5.35 Plate and base umpire responsibilities for hits to the outfield with the bases loaded.

Fly Balls

When the bases are loaded, both the plate and base umpires have specific areas of coverage and positions for fly balls. See figure 5.36 for these areas and positions.

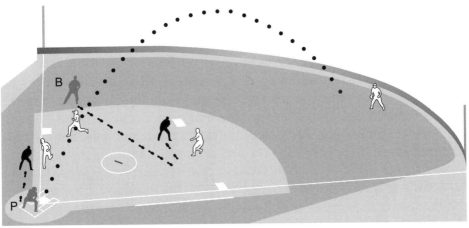

FIGURE 5.36 Plate and base umpire responsibilities for fly balls with the bases loaded.

- *Plate umpire.* Move from behind home plate to get a good view of the outfielder attempting the catch and the lead runner at third base—you are responsible for the tag-up at third. Be prepared for a play at the plate.
- *Base umpire.* Move into the infield quickly, turn and line up the runners on first and second base to call both tag-ups. Be prepared to make a call at second or third base.

Three-Umpire System

Used in both fast pitch and slow pitch, the three-umpire system is more complex than the two- (and certainly the one-) umpire system but is ideal for covering all possible plays that can occur on the field. When executed properly, the three-umpire system allows for complete coverage of all plays, no matter where they occur. The three-umpire system is generally viewed as the most enjoyable umpiring arrangement because the scope of responsibility for each crew member is reasonable but still demanding enough to keep them closely involved in the game.

This umpiring system uses a rotation plan that ensures that all bases are covered, no matter what the runner configuration. This rotation means that the plate umpire will often move to cover third base, the third-base umpire will cover second base (or even first!) and the first-base umpire frequently shifts to cover plays at the plate. Rotation always occurs in a clockwise manner, depending on the configuration of runners on base. Although this may sound complicated, once you learn the basic starting positions (standard, rotated and counterrotated) and associated movement responsibilities, it will make sense and provide for great field coverage.

Remember that in the following descriptions and diagrams, P refers to the plate umpire, B1 to the first-base umpire and B3 to the third-base umpire.

Base umpires are more likely to move into the outfield to call plays in the three-umpire system because of the extra resources on the field. This is especially true when the field is entirely enclosed, creating more fielding areas that are difficult for the plate umpire to call. When a base umpire leaves the infield in a two-umpire system, the base coverage becomes inadequate with just one umpire in the infield. But if one umpire leaves the infield in a three-umpire system, the bases are still covered by two umpires—enough to still provide strong coverage of all the bases. The rule to keep in mind with the three-umpire system is that if one of the base umpires goes to the outfield, the remaining base umpire and the plate umpire immediately revert to a two-umpire system.

There are three basic starting positions in the three-umpire system, depending on the combination of runners on the bases.

Standard Position

For the standard position with no runners on base (see figure 5.37), the plate umpire always starts behind the plate. The first-base umpire is 15 to 18 feet down the first-base line in foul territory. The first-base umpire should assume an upright and ready position. The third-base umpire is 18 to 21 feet down the third-base line in foul territory. He or she should assume an upright and ready position.

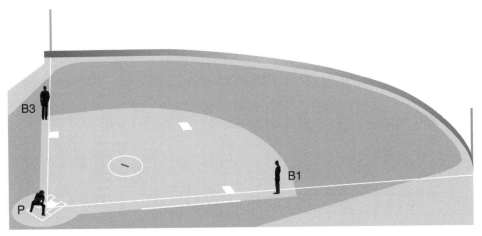

FIGURE 5.37   Standard positioning for plate and base umpires with no runners on base or a runner only on third base.

Rotated Position

The rotated position (see figure 5.38) is the basic position to any pitch when the first-base umpire is down the line at first base and the third-base umpire assumes a position behind second base. The first-base umpire should be 10 to 12 feet down the first-base line in foul territory and should assume the set position while facing the plate. The third-base umpire should be 10 to 12 feet straight out from second base toward right center field and should assume the set position while facing the plate.

Counterrotated Position

The counterrotated position (see figure 5.39) is used any time other than when there are no runners on base, a runner on first, and a runner on third. The first-base umpire should be between first and second base, about 10 to 12 feet beyond the baseline. He or she should move closer to first if there is a runner on first and not on second and should move closer to second if there is a runner on second. The first-base umpire should assume a set position while facing the plate. Note that the first-base umpire would not rotate from this position because the starting position is already ideal for all responsibilities.

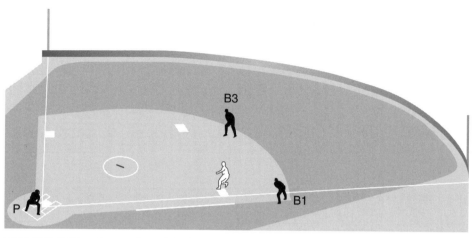

FIGURE 5.38 Rotated positioning for plate and base umpires with a runner on first base only.

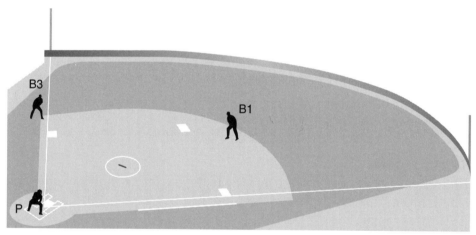

FIGURE 5.39 Counterrotated positioning for plate and base umpires for all other runner combinations (runners on first and second, runners on first and third, runner on second only, runners on second and third, bases loaded).

The third-base umpire's counterrotated position is on the third-base line in foul territory. He or she should be 15 feet down the line if there is not a runner on third and 10 to 12 feet down the line if there is a runner on third. The third-base umpire should assume a set position while facing the plate. Note that the third-base umpire may be a few feet off the line, but should always be facing the plate.

There are only three times that umpires rotate in the three-umpire system. Two of these are full rotations involving all three umpires and the other is a partial rotation involving only two of the umpires. Umpires do not rotate if any umpire goes to the outfield on a fly ball. These rotations only apply when all three umpires remain on the field.

The two full rotations are used when in the standard starting position with no runners on base or with a runner on third (see figure 5.40). The plate umpire rotates to third base and has all plays at third base. The first-base umpire pivots inside to see the batter-runner touch first. When the batter-runner advances past second base, the first-base umpire then rotates to the plate. The third-base umpire rotates into second base and has all plays at second and any play at first base after the first-base umpire has gone to the plate.

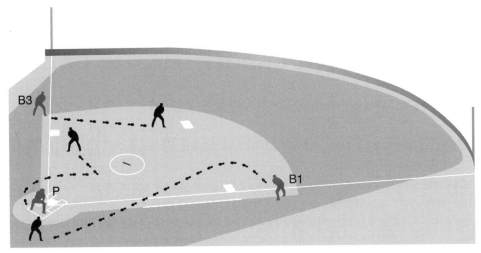

FIGURE 5.40   Full rotation with no runners on base or runner on third.

The third time umpires rotate is a partial rotation used when starting from the rotated position with a runner on first (see figure 5.41). Only the plate and first-base umpire are involved in this rotation because an umpire who does not start on the line is never involved in a rotation. In this partial rotation, the plate umpire rotates to third base and has all plays at third. The first-base umpire pivots inside and watches the batter-runner touch first. When the batter-runner advances past second base, the first-base umpire rotates to the plate. The third-base umpire will pivot inside and has all plays at second base and any play at first base after the first-base umpire has gone to the plate.

When rotating, always communicate with your partner when you are arriving at your position. Before leaving for a new position, always check that your partner is filling ahead or behind you.

Fly-Ball Coverage

As noted, base umpires are more likely to go out on fly balls in the three-umpire system. Umpires have specific areas of responsibility for when to chase a fly ball. These areas change depending on the starting

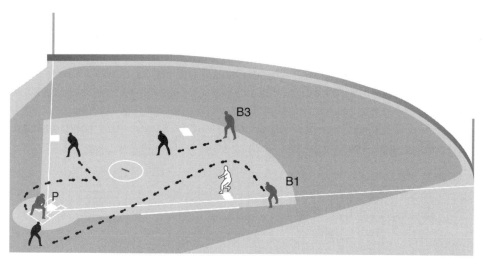

FIGURE 5.41   Partial rotation with a runner on first.

positions of the umpires. Following are umpires' fly-ball responsibilities in a three-umpire system. Note that fly-ball coverage in the three-umpire system is the same for both fast- and slow-pitch softball.

For fly balls when starting in the standard position and there are no runners on base, the plate umpire has no responsibilities, the first-base umpire is responsible for the area from the center fielder to the right-field dead-ball line, and the third-base umpire is responsible for the area from the center fielder to the left-field dead-ball line (see figure 5.42).

If the first-base umpire chases the fly ball, the plate umpire has first base and returns to the plate when the batter-runner advances past second base. The third-base umpire moves into second base and has all

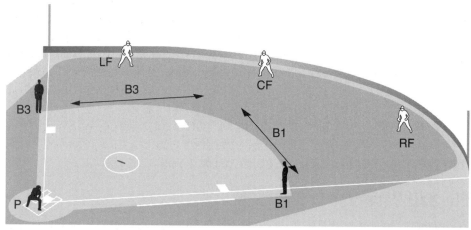

FIGURE 5.42   Fly-ball responsibility when starting in the standard position and no runners are on base.

plays at second and third. If the third-base umpire chases the fly ball, the plate umpire has the plate and the first-base umpire has all plays at first, second and third base.

For fly balls when starting in the standard position and a runner is on third (see figure 5.43), the plate umpire has no responsibilities, the first-base umpire is responsible for the area from the center fielder to the right-field dead-ball line, and the third-base umpire is responsible for the area from the center fielder to the left-field dead-ball line.

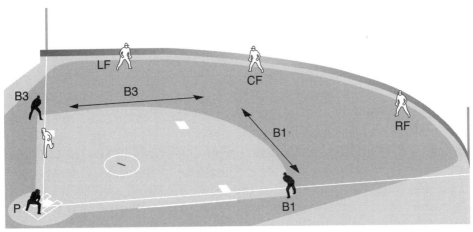

FIGURE 5.43   Fly-ball responsibility when starting in the standard position and a runner is on third.

If the first-base umpire chases the fly ball, the plate umpire has the tag-up at third and any play at third or home on the runner from third. The third-base umpire moves quickly toward first base and has all plays on the batter-runner at first, second and third. If the third-base umpire chases the fly ball, the plate umpire has the tag-up at third and any play at third or home on the runner from third. The first-base umpire pivots inside and has all plays on the batter-runner at first, second and third.

For fly balls when starting in the rotated position and there is a runner on first (see figure 5.44), the plate umpire is responsible for the area from the left fielder to the left-field dead-ball line, the first-base umpire is responsible for the area from the right fielder to the right-field dead-ball line and the third-base umpire is responsible for the area from the right fielder to the left fielder.

If the first-base umpire chases the fly ball, the plate umpire has the tag-up at first base, takes the lead runner at third and all plays at the plate. The third-base umpire pivots inside and has all plays at second, any play at first base after the plate umpire leaves and the batter-runner at third. If the third-base umpire chases the fly ball, the plate umpire has the lead runner at

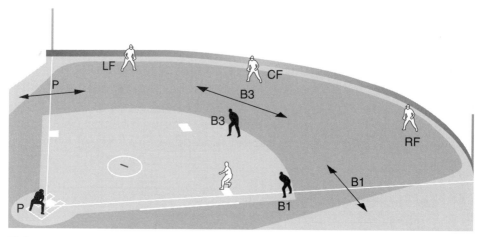

FIGURE 5.44   Fly-ball responsibility when starting in the rotated position and a runner is on first.

third-base and all plays at the plate. The first-base umpire has the tag-up at first base, all plays at first and second and the batter-runner at third base.

For fly balls, when starting in the counterrotated position and there are runners anywhere except first or third only (see figure 5.45), the plate umpire is responsible for the area from the right fielder to the right-field dead-ball line, the first-base umpire is responsible for the area from the right fielder to the left fielder and the third-base umpire is responsible for the area from the left fielder to the left-field dead-ball line.

If the first-base umpire chases the fly ball and there is a runner on third, the third-base umpire has tag-ups at first and second. If there are runners on first and second, the third-base umpire has the tag up at first. The third-base umpire has all plays at first and second and trail runners at third.

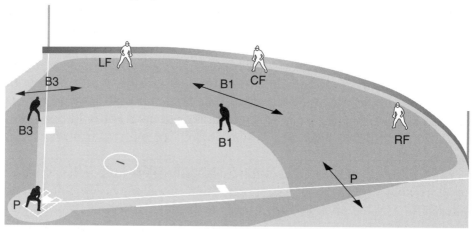

FIGURE 5.45   Fly-ball responsibility when starting in the counterrotated position and runners are anywhere except first or third only.

If the third-base umpire chases the fly ball and there is a runner on third, the first-base umpire has the tag-ups at first and second. If there are runners on first and second, the first-base umpire has the tag-up at first. The first-base umpire has all plays at first and second and trail runners at third.

In addition to this, no matter who chases the fly ball, the plate umpire has all tag-ups at third when there is a runner on third. If there are runners on first and second, with the third-base umpire chasing a fly ball, the plate umpire has the tag-up at second. The plate umpire has all plays at the plate and lead runner at third.

On balls hit directly at the center fielder, the first-base umpire is generally given the "right of first refusal." The first-base umpire has the most imminent play and must make a decision quickly. The third-base umpire can more easily adjust. For example, if the third-base umpire starts for the outfield and notices that the first-base umpire has also started, the third-base umpire can simply change course and move toward second base. Conversely, if the third-base umpire starts toward second base and notices that the first-base umpire is not going out on the ball, he or she can easily adjust and parallel the flight of the ball out to the center fielder. It is the responsibility of the third-base umpire to ensure that two umpires never chase the same ball, thereby leaving the plate umpire as the only umpire on the infield.

Following are ideal positioning guides for every base-runner situation. Note that you may need to deviate somewhat from these recommendations depending on the game situation you are in to avoid interfering with a play. For example, if the defensive team makes a stronger-than-usual shift for a left-handed batter, the first-base umpire may need to move to get out of the way of the shifted shortstop or second-base fielder. Use good judgment, know your responsibilities and keep the current game situation in mind, and you will be on top of every play you need to call.

No Runners on Base

At the start of play, the base umpires assume positions outside the base lines about 15 to 18 feet behind first and third base.

Base Hit to Outfield

When there are no runners on base, the plate umpire (P), first-base umpire (B1) and third-base umpire (B3) have specific areas of coverage and positions on a base hit to the outfield. See figure 5.46 for these areas and positions.

- *P coverage.* Move into the infield toward the pitching circle. Release toward third base for a possible call if the runner attempts to advance to third.

- *B1 coverage.* Pivot (or buttonhook) inside the diamond and look to second base to make sure B3 is covering second. If so, when the batter-runner advances past second base, release and move toward home plate in case there is a play at home on the batter-runner. When covering home plate, move to the rear of the right-hand batter's box for a good view of the plate.

- *B3 coverage.* Move inside the diamond toward second base to cover any play there. Watch to make sure the plate umpire is covering third base.

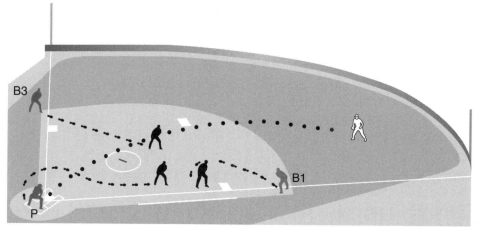

FIGURE 5.46   Plate and base umpire responsibilities for a base hit to the outfield with no runners on base.

Hits to Infield

When there are no runners on base, the plate umpire (P), first-base umpire (B1) and third-base umpire (B3) have specific areas of coverage and positions when a ball is hit to the infield. See figure 5.47 for these areas and positions.

- *P coverage.* Trail the batter-runner to first base and be prepared to cover third base if the batter-runner advances to third.

- *B1 coverage.* Move into fair territory no more than 45 degrees off the line and 15 to 18 feet from from first for the play at the base. If the batter-runner advances past second base, move quickly to the plate.

- *B3 coverage.* Move directly into the field to a position 10 to 12 feet on the infield side of second base. Take all plays at second and any play at first after the B1 has left for the plate.

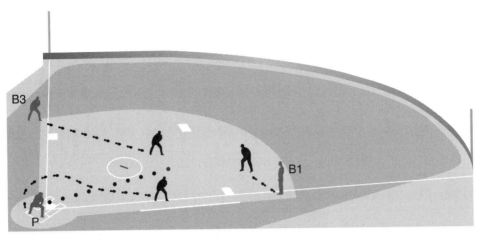

FIGURE 5.47   Plate and base umpire responsibilities for hits to the infield with no runners on base.

Runner on First

When there is a runner on first, the base umpires start in a rotated position with the first-base umpire down the line at first base and the third-base umpire assuming a position behind second base.

Base Hit to Outfield

When there is a runner on first base, the plate umpire (P), first-base umpire (B1) and third-base umpire (B3) have specific areas of coverage and positions on a base hit to the outfield. See figure 5.48 for these areas and positions.

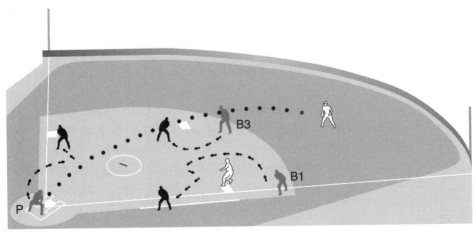

FIGURE 5.48   Plate and base umpire responsibilities for a base hit to the outfield with a runner on first base.

- *P coverage.* Move toward third base to prepare for a possible call there.
- *B1 coverage.* Pivot inside the diamond and watch the batter-runner touch first base. When the runner from first advances past second base, release and rotate to home plate for any calls. Position yourself at the rear of the right-hand batter's box.
- *B3 coverage.* Pivot inside the diamond to cover any plays at second base. Be alert for any possible calls at first if B1 has rotated home.

Hits to Infield

When there is a runner on first base, the plate umpire (P), first-base umpire (B1) and third-base umpire (B3) have specific areas of coverage and positions on hits to the infield. See figure 5.49 for these areas and positions.

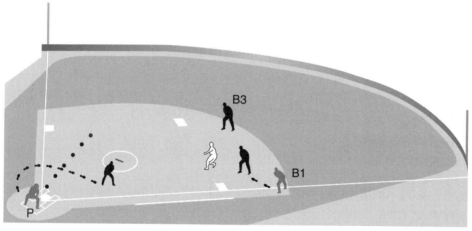

FIGURE 5.49 Plate and base umpire responsibilities for hits to the infield with a runner on first base.

- *P coverage.* Trail the batter-runner 15 feet to first base and be prepared to quickly cover third base if the runner from first advances to third.
- *B1 coverage.* Move into fair territory no more than 45 degrees off the line and 15 to 18 feet from first for the play at first base. If the runner from first advances past second base, move quickly to the plate.
- *B3 coverage.* Stay outside the diamond and take all plays at second base and any plays at first base after B1 has gone to the plate.

Runner on Second

When there is a runner on second, umpires should start in a counterrotated position with the third-base umpire down the line at third base and the first-base umpire assuming a position behind the second-base player.

Base Hit to Outfield

When there is a runner on second base, the plate umpire (P), first-base umpire (B1) and third-base umpire (B3) have specific areas of coverage and positions on a base hit to the outfield. See figure 5.50 for these areas and positions.

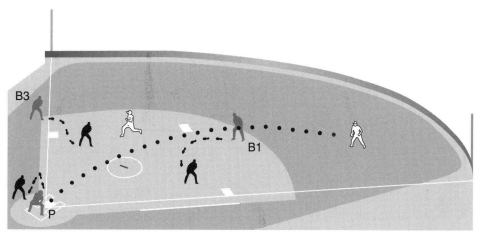

FIGURE 5.50   Plate and base umpire responsibilities for a base hit to the outfield with a runner on second base.

- *P coverage.* Remain at the plate in foul territory and prepare for a play at the plate.
- *B1 coverage.* Pivot inside the diamond and prepare to make calls at first or second base.
- *B3 coverage.* Pivot inside the diamond and make calls at third base.

Hits to Infield

When there is a runner on second base, the plate umpire (P), first-base umpire (B1) and third-base umpire (B3) have specific areas of coverage and positions on hits to the infield. See figure 5.51 for these areas and positions.

- *P coverage.* Drop back to a first-base line extended position in foul territory. Watch the play at first base and be prepared for a play at the plate.
- *B1 coverage.* If the first play is at first base, stay outside the diamond and move to the same position you would when coming off the line for a play at first base. If the first play is at second base, move straight forward toward the base line to make the call. You have all plays at second and first base. Be aware of crossing or being in throwing lanes.

- *B3 coverage.* Stay outside the diamond and make all calls at third base. Adjust your positioning for runners coming into the base and for those who have rounded the base. Since you have no responsibilities at second and there is help ahead, you may use foul, as well as fair territory, to make calls.

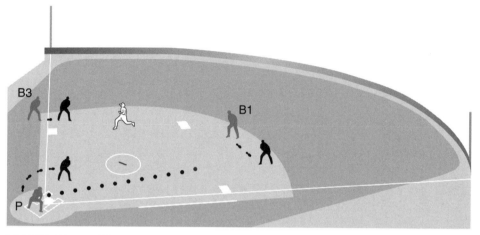

FIGURE 5.51   Plate and base umpire responsibilities for hits to the infield with a runner on second base.

Runner on Third

When there is a runner on third, the starting positions for the base umpires should be the basic position down the foul lines.

Base Hit to Outfield

When there is a runner on third base, the plate umpire (P), first-base umpire (B1) and third-base umpire (B3) have specific areas of coverage and positions on a base hit to the outfield. See figure 5.52 for these areas and positions.

- *P coverage.* Remain at the plate in foul territory. After watching the runner from third touch home, release and go to third base to get positioned inside the diamond for any possible calls at third. When you move to third base, look to make sure the first-base umpire has moved to cover home plate.

- *B1 coverage.* Pivot inside the diamond and watch the batter-runner touch first base. Be prepared to take the batter-runner to second if the runner from third has not scored. If the runner from third has scored and B3 is covering second, when the batter-runner advances past second base, move quickly to home plate for any plays at the plate. Position yourself in the right-hand batter's box for the best angle on home plate.

- *B3 coverage*. Make sure the runner from third has committed to home plate. If not, stay at third base. If so, move inside the diamond for any play at second base or at first base after B1 has gone to the plate. Look to make sure the plate umpire is covering third base.

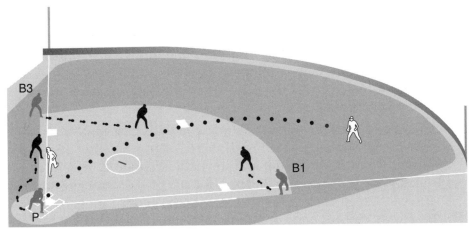

FIGURE 5.52   Plate and base umpire responsibilities for a base hit to the outfield with a runner on third base.

Hits to Infield

When there is a runner on third base, the plate umpire (P), first-base umpire (B1) and third-base umpire (B3) have specific areas of coverage and positions on hits to the infield. See figure 5.53 for these areas and positions.

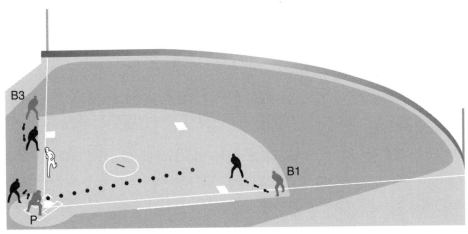

FIGURE 5.53   Plate and base umpire responsibilities for hits to the infield with a runner on third base.

- *P coverage.* Remain at the plate in foul territory. Use the first-base line extended to watch the play at first base. Take the play on the runner from third at home. If the batter-runner is safe at first and the runner from third has scored (such as on an overthrow at first base), move quickly to third base for any play at third on the batter-runner. Make sure B3 has rotated into the diamond and that B1 is covering home.

- *B1 coverage.* Move into fair territory for a play at first base. Be prepared to take the batter-runner to second if the runner from third has not scored. If there is a misplay that allows the runner from third to score, the batter-runner is to be safe, and B3 covering second should move to cover the plate when the batter-runner advances past second base.

- *B3 coverage.* Stay outside the diamond at third base for any possible play on the runner from third. If there is a misplay that allows the runner from third to score and the batter-runner to be safe, move quickly and directly to second base for any play on the batter-runner at second. If B1 is already moving with the batter-runner to second base, stay at third and communicate to the plate umpire, "I've got third!"

Runners on First and Second

When there are runners on first and second, the base umpires should start in a counterrotated position.

Base Hit to Outfield

When there are runners on first and second base, the plate umpire (P), first-base umpire (B1) and third-base umpire (B3) have specific areas of coverage and positions on a base hit to the outfield. See figure 5.54 for these areas and positions. It should also be noted that no rotation is made when the first-base umpire begins play at second base.

- *P coverage.* Remain at home plate in foul territory and prepare for a play at home.

- *B1 coverage.* Pivot inside the diamond and prepare to make calls at first or second base.

- *B3 coverage.* Pivot inside the diamond and make any call at third base.

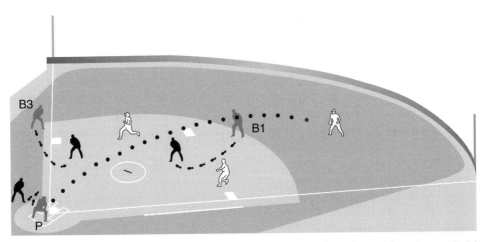

FIGURE 5.54   Plate and base umpire responsibilities for a base hit to the outfield with runners on first and second base.

Hits to Infield

When there are runners on first and second base, the plate umpire (P), first-base umpire (B1) and third-base umpire (B3) have specific areas of coverage and positions on hits to the infield. See figure 5.55 for these areas and positions.

- *P coverage.* Drop back to a first-base line extended position to watch the play at first base. Be prepared for any play at the plate.
- *B1 coverage.* Stay outside the diamond and take all plays at second and first. Let the throw guide your movement and get in a good position for a play at either base. If a double play is attempted, take

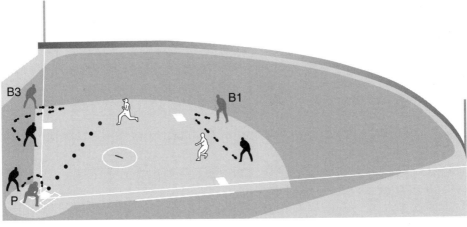

FIGURE 5.55   Plate and base umpire responsibilities for hits to the infield with runners on first and second base.

one step at second base, then quickly move to a position for the call at first. Note that this is one of the few times it is okay for umpires to make a call and signal on the move.

- *B3 coverage.* Move into fair territory, staying outside the diamond. Take all plays at third base. Adjust your distance and angle from the play for a force or a tag. Since you have no responsibilities at second and there is help ahead, you may use foul as well as fair territory when adjusting for the call.

Runners on First and Third

When there are runners on first and third, the base umpires will start in a counterrotated position.

Base Hit to Outfield

When there are runners on first and third base, the plate umpire (P), first-base umpire (B1) and third-base umpire (B3) have specific areas of coverage and positions on a base hit to the outfield. See figure 5.56 for these areas and positions. It should also be noted that no rotation is made when the first-base umpire begins play at second base.

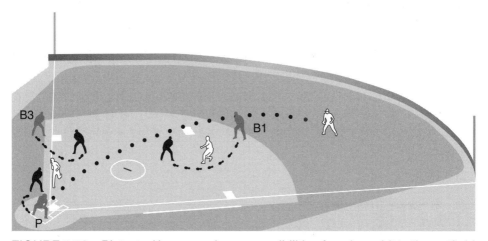

FIGURE 5.56   Plate and base umpire responsibilities for a base hit to the outfield with runners on first and third base.

- *P coverage.* Remain at the plate in foul territory and prepare to call any play at home plate.
- *B1 coverage.* Pivot inside the diamond and prepare to make any calls at first or second base.
- *B3 coverage.* Pivot inside the diamond and make any call at third base.

Hits to Infield

When there are runners on first and third base, the plate umpire (P), first-base umpire (B1) and third-base umpire (B3) have specific areas of coverage and positions on hits to the infield. See figure 5.57 for these areas and positions.

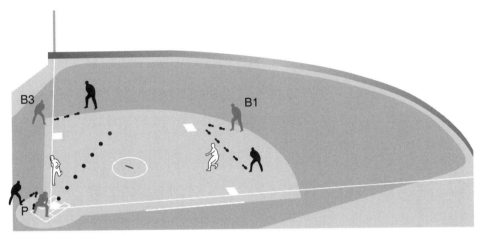

FIGURE 5.57 Plate and base umpire responsibilities for hits to the infield with runners on first and third base.

- *P coverage.* Drop back to a first-base line extended position in foul territory and watch the play at first base. Take all plays at the plate.
- *B1 coverage.* Stay outside the diamond and take all plays at second and first. Let the throw guide your movement and get into a good position for a play at either base. If a double play is attempted, take one step at second base, then quickly move to a position for the call at first. Note that this is one of the few times it is OK for umpires to make a call and signal on the move. If the initial play is at first and there is a subsequent play behind the runner at second, move straight forward toward the base line to call this play.
- *B3 coverage.* Move into fair territory and stay outside the diamond. Take all plays at third base. Since you have no responsibilities at second and there is help ahead, you may use foul as well as fair territory when adjusting for your plays.

Runners on Second and Third

When there are runners on second and third, the base umpires will start in a counterrotated position prior to the pitch.

Base Hit to Outfield

When there are runners on second and third base, the plate umpire (P), first-base umpire (B1) and third-base umpire (B3) have specific areas of coverage and positions on a base hit to the outfield. See figure 5.58 for these areas and positions.

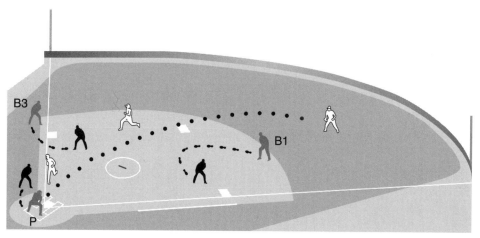

FIGURE 5.58   Plate and base umpire responsibilities for a base hit to the outfield with runners on second and third base.

- *P coverage.* Remain at home plate in foul territory. Take all plays at the plate.
- *B1 coverage.* Pivot inside the diamond and be prepared to make any calls at first or second base.
- *B3 coverage.* Pivot inside the diamond and make any call at third base.

Hits to Infield

When there are runners on second and third base, the plate umpire (P), first-base umpire (B1) and third-base umpire (B3) have specific areas of coverage and positions on hits to the infield. See figure 5.59 for these areas and positions.

- *P coverage.* Drop back to a first-base line extended position to watch the play at first base. Be prepared for and take all calls at the plate.
- *B1 coverage.* Stay outside the diamond and take all plays at first or second base. If the initial play is at first base, move to a position similar to the one you would assume when coming off the line for a play at first. If the initial play is behind the runner at second base, move straight forward toward the base line. Be aware of being in a throwing lane.

- *B3 coverage.* Stay outside the diamond. Move either into fair territory or up the line in foul territory as the play dictates. Take all plays at third base.

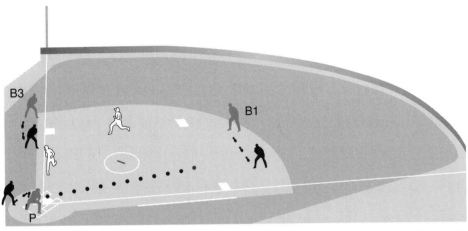

FIGURE 5.59   Plate and base umpire responsibilities for hits to the infield with runners on second and third base.

Bases Loaded

When the bases are loaded, the base umpires will start in a counterrotated position, prior to the pitch.

Base Hit to Outfield

When the bases are loaded, the plate umpire (P), first-base umpire (B1) and third-base umpire (B3) have specific areas of coverage and positions on a base hit to the outfield. See figure 5.60 for these areas and positions.

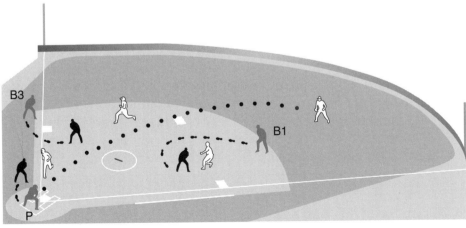

FIGURE 5.60   Plate and base umpire responsibilities for a base hit to the outfield with the bases loaded.

- *P coverage.* Remain at the plate in foul territory and get ready for a play at home.
- *B1 coverage.* Pivot inside the diamond and make any calls at first or second base.
- *B3 coverage.* Pivot inside the diamond and make any call at third base.

Hits to Infield

When the bases are loaded, the plate umpire (P), first-base umpire (B1) and third-base umpire (B3) have specific areas of coverage and positions on hits to the infield. See figure 5.61 for these areas and positions.

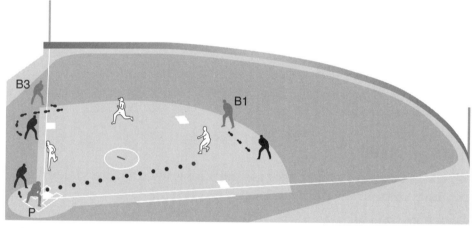

FIGURE 5.61   Plate and base umpire responsibilities for hits to the infield with the bases loaded.

- *P coverage.* Remain at the plate in foul territory. If the initial play is at the plate, increase your distance from the play for the force play. If the initial play is at first base, assume a first-base line extended position to watch the play at first and see the runner from third touch home plate. Take all plays at the plate.
- *B1 coverage.* Stay on the outside of the diamond and take all plays at first and second base. Let the throw guide your movement and get a good position for the type of play at either base. If the initial play is at first base, move to a position similar to the one you would assume when coming off the line for a play at first. If a double play is attempted, take one step at second base and quickly move to a position for the call at first.
- *B3 coverage.* Stay outside the diamond and move into fair territory or up the line in foul territory as the play dictates. Take all plays at third base.

Mechanics Between Innings
(Two- and Three-Umpire Systems)

The last out of the inning has been made, so now what do you do? Get a hot dog? No, not quite. Following are recommended positions to assume while waiting for the inning changeover.

Plate Umpire

Position yourself approximately 20 feet from home plate near the line in foul territory, facing the infield. You should alternate between the first- and third-base foul lines by always taking a position on the line on the side of the team going into the field to play defense (see figure 5.62). Alternating this way keeps you from unintentionally spending more time closer to one team than the other, which could potentially convey the impression of favoritism. This position also allows you to monitor the on-deck batter, ensuring she is on the on-deck taking her practice swing.

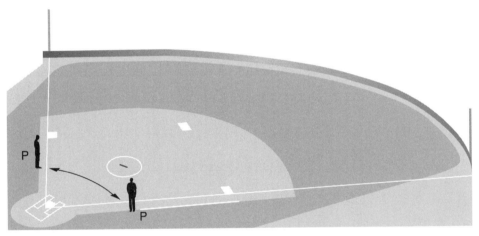

FIGURE 5.62   Plate umpire position between innings.

Base Umpire

Position yourself at the edge of the outfield in fair territory, facing the infield (see figure 5.63). If necessary, keep players moving to speed the changeover with a friendly, "Hustle up!"

In a two-umpire system, the first-base umpire is responsible for brushing off the pitcher's plate after the last out of each half-inning. In a three-umpire system, the third-base umpire is responsible for cleaning the pitcher's plate after the last out of each half-inning. This arrangement need not be a hard-and-fast rule—if the umpire responsible for cleaning the pitcher's plate is in the outfield on the last out of the inning, another umpire should brush off the plate.

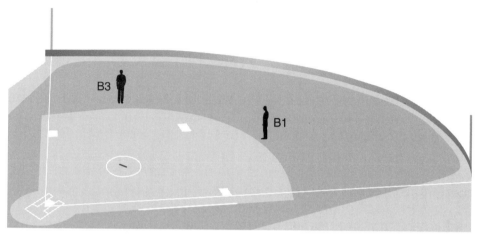

Figure 5.63   Base umpire positions between innings.

PART III

APPLYING THE RULES

CHAPTER 6

PROCEDURES, TERMS AND CONDUCT

As a batter steps up to the plate, you notice her uniform number does not match what was submitted on the lineup card. Do you allow the batter to hit? A batter deliberately removes her helmet while running to first base. Do you need to call the batter out? On a deep fly ball, the left fielder drops the ball while attempting to throw to second base. How do you decide if it is a legal catch? How many additional conferences is each team allowed if a game goes into extra innings?

All these questions and more are reviewed in this chapter through play situations developed as a result of thousands of games of umpiring experience. These cases are the next-best thing to firsthand experience and should be studied closely to understand the nuances that cause a ruling to go one way or another. The cases have been selected to illustrate commonly occurring situations in high school softball but are by no means exhaustive. The *NFHS Softball Case Book* contains hundreds of additional cases that will help you learn your craft.

The answers to the following case challenges are provided at the end of the chapter. Consider each case and determine what your ruling would be, then check the official rulings to see if you know your stuff! You should keep your *NFHS Softball Rules Book* handy for reference as you work through the case examples to look up the official line on any ruling that does not make sense.

The cases in this chapter cover the following rules:

- Rule 1: Field and Equipment
- Rule 2: Definitions
- Rule 3: Players, Substitutions and Coaches

The remaining seven rules are covered in chapters 7, 8 and 9.

Rule 1: Field and Equipment

Following are a few scenarios that illustrate common situations you will likely encounter on the field. Consider how you'd respond in each situation, and check your judgments against the answers beginning on page 138 at the end of the chapter.

Helmets and Masks

Batting helmets may be the most important piece of equipment on the field, and as an umpire, you need to take a role in ensuring they are worn correctly whenever required by the rules.

A batting helmet bearing the permanent NOCSAE stamp and exterior warning label is mandatory for each batter, on-deck batter, players/ students in the coaches' boxes, runners and retired runners. Similarly, the catcher, whether catching or warming up a pitcher in the game, must use a catcher's helmet and mask displaying the NOCSAE stamp and warning on the helmet. The exterior warning label may be affixed to the helmet in either sticker form or embossed form (at the point of manufacture) and must be clearly visible. Non-adult bat/ball shaggers must also wear batting helmets while in the live-ball area, even if the ball is dead.

The batting helmet must have extended, dual earflaps that cover both the ears and the temples. Batting helmets that are broken, cracked, dented or that have been altered are prohibited from use. All helmets should fit well. A helmet that does not fit correctly may not protect the wearer properly.

A commercially manufactured face mask may be attached to a batting helmet, provided it is attached by the manufacturer. Similarly, a face mask may be attached to a helmet that was not originally manufactured with one, provided the attachment procedure is approved by the manufacturer. If a pitcher (or any defensive player) wears a batting helmet, its outer covering must have a nonglare surface.

CASE 1: Player Removes Helmet
With one out and a runner on first, a batter hits a ground ball to the center fielder. While advancing to first base, the batter deliberately removes her helmet. Is this a violation of the rules?

CASE 2: The NOCSAE Official Stamp
You observe that a batter is standing in the batter's box wearing a protective helmet that does not have a permanent NOCSAE stamp, or a batter hits safely and reaches first base and the first-base umpire notices that the warning label is missing from the helmet. Do you address this issue after the game with the team's coach, or do you need to take more immediate action?

Softballs

Just as with other game equipment, there are regulations as to the compression rating, circumference and weight of softballs. Game balls must be white or optic yellow; only one color of ball may be used throughout a game. All balls must have the NFHS Authenticating Mark on the cover.

For slow-pitch softball, states may decide to use 11- or 12-inch-circumference softballs. Fast-pitch games always use 12-inch-circumference softballs. Other important ball specifications include coefficient of restitution (COR), compression and weight. COR refers to an index of how active a ball is when hit by a bat. Compression refers to how much physical "give" a softball has when weight pressure is placed on it. Consult the *NFHS Softball Rules Book* for detailed specifications for legal softballs and be aware they are subject to change.

Softballs used in a game should be white or optic yellow and should be labeled with the NFHS Authenticating Mark.

CASE 3: *White or Optic Yellow Softballs*

During the pregame conference, the home team presents white game balls to you as the plate umpire. The visiting team is from a neighboring state where optic yellow balls are used and requests that they be used in the game. The home team also indicates a preference for the yellow balls but believes the state has not approved them for game use. Since both teams prefer the yellow ball, can the visiting team provide yellow balls for use in the game?

Bats

The softball bat must be a smooth cylinder with a knob at the end of the handle. A legal bat is able to pass through a 2 1/4-inch-diameter bat ring (in other words, the bat cannot be wider than 2 1/4 inches in diameter at its thickest point) and must not exceed 34 inches in length. A bat ring is a "must have" piece of equipment for every umpire. All bats must meet the specifications in the *NFHS Softball Rules Book* to be allowed in the game, which includes meeting the correct Amateur Softball Association (ASA) Bat Performance Standard.

CASE 4: Wrapped Bat Handle

As B1 steps into the batter's box, you notice the bat handle is wrapped with (a) smooth plastic tape or (b) athletic tape. In either case, is the bat legal or illegal?

Nonregulation Facilities

No two fields are exactly the same, requiring your pregame field inspection to be rigorous. Be aware of field regulations, and make every effort to ensure you are aware of any anomalies before the game begins.

CASE 5: Incorrectly Set Pitcher's Plate

In the top of the first inning, the pitcher has great difficulty throwing strikes, and the offensive team scores several runs as a result of four walks. At the inning changeover, the other team's pitcher complains that the pitcher's plate is not set at the correct distance from the plate. When you measure it, you discover that she is right—the pitcher's plate is almost a foot too far from the plate. Do you negate the runs scored in the previous inning? Do you leave the plate in its incorrect position for the bottom half of the inning to even things up?

Rule 2: Definitions

Following are important game-play definitions and cases that illustrate their application. You are likely to encounter situations where you need to explain a rule in terms of the official definition, so make sure you know these and all other definitions included in the *NFHS Softball Rules Book*. Consider how you'd respond in each situation, and check your judgments against the answers beginning on page 139 at the end of the chapter.

Appeals

An appeal play is defined as "a play or rule violation on which the umpire does not make a ruling until requested to by a coach or player," and the appeal is the actual request for a ruling. Appeals can change the outcome of a game, negating an advantage that was illegally or inadvertently achieved. But an appeal may also be without merit, requiring it to be rejected. Appeals put you, the umpire, in the hot seat to solve a dispute, so you should know how to handle them and should understand what occurred in the situation under dispute.

CASE 6: Runner Misses a Base

With a runner on third and one out, a batter hits safely. The runner from third watches the ball, but does not touch home plate. The catcher calls for the ball, tags the runner from third and appeals that she missed the plate. The umpire rules the runner out. The catcher then throws to third to get the batter sliding into the base. Does the run count? Is the play at third base live?

Catches

A catch occurs when a fielder uses her hand(s) and/or glove to securely gain possession of a batted, pitched or thrown ball. In establishing the validity of the catch, you must determine whether the fielder holds the ball long enough to prove she has control of it and that her release of the ball is voluntary and intentional (did she drop it or throw it?). If the fielder makes the catch but drops the ball, either in transferring it to the throwing hand or in making a throw, the ball is ruled caught.

CASE 7: A Catch or a Dropped Ball?

In the seventh inning, a batter hits a deep fly ball to the center fielder. The center fielder gets the ball in her glove but drops it as she falls to the ground and rolls over, when she collides with another fielder or a wall, or when she starts to throw to the infield cutoff. Was the ball caught?

Pregame and Charged Conferences

A pregame conference is a meeting involving the umpires, coaches and team captains near home plate prior to a game. The meeting should begin approximately five minutes prior to the game, before the home team takes the field. The purpose of this conference is to exchange and verify lineup cards, discuss ground rules and emphasize proper behavior.

A charged conference can be offensive or defensive. An offensive charged conference occurs when a coach requests time to talk to the batter, runners or other team personnel. One offensive conference is allowed each half inning. A defensive charged conference occurs when a representative from the dugout requests time to talk to a defensive player. Three defensive charged conferences are allowed in a seven-inning game. All three can be taken in one inning, or they can be spread out, but they cannot be carried over into extra innings. One defensive charged conference is allowed in each extra inning.

CASE 8: Pitcher's Conference

After walking two consecutive batters, the pitcher's coach calls time and takes the field to talk with her, or the third baseman walks to the pitcher's area to talk with the pitcher. Are these conferences legal, and should they be charged?

Interference and Obstruction

There are several types of interference: runner, batter, on-deck batter, coach or team personnel, umpire, spectator or offensive equipment. The most common is runner interference. In basic terms, a runner cannot confuse, hinder or impede a fielder fielding a batted ball or interfere with a fielder throwing the ball. Interference also occurs if a runner intentionally creates contact with any fielder with or without the ball, in or out of the baseline.

Obstruction occurs when a member of the defensive team hinders or impedes a batter's attempt to make contact with a pitched ball or the progress of a runner who is legally running bases unless the fielder is in possession of the ball or is fielding a batted ball. The defensive player's act may be intentional or unintentional, physical or verbal.

CASE 9: Faked Tag

The shortsthop fakes a tag as a runner approaches second base. The runner decides to continue on to third base, where she is thrown out. Did the shortsthop commit obstruction? Do you grant the runner third base?

Rule 3: Players, Substitutions and Coaches

Following are several cases that illustrate important points relating to the actions of coaches, injured players and unsporting acts. Consider how you'd respond in each situation, and check your judgments against the answers beginning on page 140 at the end of the chapter.

Player Positions and Lineups

As the plate umpire, you need to manage the lineup cards for both teams carefully and be vigilant about the names and numbers of player substitutes throughout the game. Base umpires should be cognizant of lineups as well and should help the plate umpire watch for possible lineup or other violations. The *NFHS Softball Rules Book* includes numerous rules pertaining to player lineup and position management, and a few of the most common are illustrated below.

CASE 10: Wrong Uniform Number

A player named Brown, officially listed in the batting order as wearing uniform No. 4, is actually wearing No. 21. After Brown reaches base in the third inning, the coach of the opposing team appeals to you, saying that Brown is batting out of order (because the lineup states No. 4 should be batting when, in fact, Brown's uniform makes it appear that No. 21 is batting). What is the correct call?

CASE 11: An Unlisted Substitute

You are the plate umpire in a close tournament game between two rivals. In the third inning, a substitute reports to you, but her name is not on the lineup card even though she was on the bench at the start of the game, or the substitute arrived *after* the game started and therefore was not on the lineup card. Do you allow her to play in these situations?

Uniforms

Very specific regulations exist to ensure that neither team gains an advantage or creates a safety risk as a result of the color, size or other aspect of the uniform (including how a legal uniform is worn). An unfair advantage could theoretically occur as a result of something as simple as an article of clothing with the wrong colors that confuses the opposing team momentarily during a close play. Jewelry, plastic visors, splints and casts are all hazards and thus are governed closely by the rules. Uniform rules should be strictly and consistently enforced.

If a uniform violation can be corrected in a reasonable amount of time (as determined by you, the umpire), the violation may be remedied before the player participates in the game. If the violation cannot be corrected quickly, the player may participate in the game, but you need to notify the coach of the violating team that an official uniform violation has occurred, and you must also make the state association aware of the infraction. In other words, you should not prohibit a player from playing the game for a uniform violation that can't be remedied but should make sure the violation is reported to league authorities so it gets rectified before the next game.

CASE 12: Uniform Variations
Upon arrival at the field, you immediately notice that eight members of a team are wearing red shorts and the ninth player is wearing a red skirt; later in the game, you observe a coach or player-coach wearing a jacket while in the coaching box; a player asks to wear a jacket over her uniform while running the bases. Do any of these situations create a problem you need to address?

CASE 13: Uniform Numbers, Logos and Patches
While you are walking the field before the game, you notice that players on team A are wearing numbers on the backs of their jerseys that look to be less than 6 inches high. What do you do?

Medical Equipment

Players commonly take the field wearing some type of medical gear, ranging from medical-alert bracelets to splints or casts. Although cosmetic jewelry is not allowed, medical symbols and equipment are allowed in certain cases.

CASE 14: Jewelry and Medical Symbols

You notice that a runner has tape on her wrist that is bulky. You inquire and are told it is covering a medical-alert bracelet. Is this legal?

Substitution

A substitute may replace a player, including the pitcher, when the ball is dead or time has been called. The substitute or coach must report to the plate umpire at the time of the change by stating the name and uniform number of the player entering the game and identifying the player being replaced.

CASE 15: Substitution During an At Bat

A batter has a count of one ball and two strikes when her coach attempts to substitute a pinch hitter for her. Can the coach legally make this substitution after the at bat has already begun?

CASE 16: Reentering the Game

Player Jones starts in center field and is scheduled to bat second in the batting order. In the second inning, Smith replaces Jones. Subsequently, the coach attempts to reenter Jones as catcher and have her bat in the eighth position. Does this qualify as a legal substitution?

Designated Player (DP)

In fast pitch, a hitter (DP) may be designated to bat for any one starting defensive player (FLEX) and all subsequent substitutes for that player in the game. A DP must be identified on the lineup card presented to the plate umpire and the official scorekeeper prior to the start of the game. No team is required to use a DP, but failure to declare a DP prior to the game precludes the use of one in that game.

The DP may play defense for the FLEX. This would force the FLEX to leave the game, and the team would have to play with nine players. The DP may play defense for any other player in the batting order. That player would not leave the game but would continue to bat in the same batting position—she just would not be playing defense. The team would still be playing with ten players. The FLEX can only play offense for the DP; this would force the DP to leave the game, and the team would have to play with nine players. Both the DP and FLEX may be withdrawn and reentered once. Their substitutes become the DP and FLEX, respectively.

The DP must play offense to be considered in the game. The FLEX must play defense to be considered in the game. The DP and FLEX can be on defense at the same time, but they cannot be on offense at the same time.

CASE 17: DP and the Reentry Rule

The DP, batting in the second position for the starting FLEX, who is playing first base, desires to play first base when her team goes on defense.

Can the DP enter the game as a defensive fielder? Does she have to enter for the FLEX to play first base?

Injured Player

Minimizing risk to all game participants is part of your job as umpire. You always have authority to suspend play immediately if in your judgment further play may jeopardize a participant's safety.

CASE 18: Bleeding Player

A runner slides into second base and scrapes her knee, causing it to bleed slightly. Must you remove the bleeding player from the game immediately, or can you wait until the player scores or the inning is over?

Unsporting Acts

All participants in interscholastic competition, including players, coaches and umpires, are expected to exhibit sporting behavior and fair play. As umpire, you will occasionally be required to deal with and penalize unsporting behavior, which might include a range of situations:

- Uniforms not worn properly—jersey not tucked in, sleeves rolled under and caps worn backward
- Exposed undergarments of different colors by players on the same team
- Use of equipment in a manner other than intended (for example, throwing a bat)
- Verbal insults
- Illegal equipment put into play after the equipment check
- Coaches knowingly using illegal players or substitutes
- Coaching tactics that put players at risk

Administrators, coaches and you should take an active role in ensuring appropriate conduct by all participants. Behaviors and strategies should be within the rules of the game and should always reflect the spirit of fair play.

Umpires and other game personnel should know when to recognize unsporting acts, such as a uniform not being worn properly.

CASE 19: Player Throws a Bat

After hitting a line drive toward the third baseman, a batter throws her bat, and it strikes the catcher or umpire. (a) What is the penalty if the act was judged to be intentional? (b) If the act was judged to be unintentional?

Answers

In this section, we've provided the correct answers to each situation. Check your responses to see how you did.

Case 1: Player Removes Helmet

A team warning shall be issued to the coach of the player who removed her helmet when the first offense occurs unless the batted ball enters dead-ball territory without being touched by a fielder or, after being touched, goes directly into dead-ball territory. In other words, if the ball is hit in such a way that the play has clearly gone dead, there is no penalty for removing a batting helmet. Once a team has received a warning for a player illegally removing her helmet, any subsequent offenders on that same team shall be restricted to the dugout/bench for the duration of the game.

Helmets are an extremely important piece of protective equipment—players should never remove them during a live play. Minimizing risk always takes precedence over competition, and an important part of your job is doing what you can to reduce player risk.

Case 2: The NOCSAE Official Stamp

In both instances, you must immediately require the player to secure a proper helmet. The coach should be warned that the next player who does not wear a legal batting helmet shall be restricted to the dugout/bench for the duration of the game.

There is no room for rules interpretation when it comes to helmets—everyone must strictly follow the rules. Replacement equipment should be sought the moment you notice a problem. That goes for batters, players in the on-deck circle, ball shaggers and players/students in the coaches' boxes at first and third or anywhere in live territory. If you notice a player without a helmet between innings or before play has started, you may direct the player to obtain and wear a helmet without penalty.

Case 3: White or Optic Yellow Softballs

Yes, the visiting team can provide the optic yellow balls for the game as long as the home coach agrees and the plate umpire approves the decision.

The state association does not govern which type of ball is used. Instead, the decision is made on a game-by-game basis by the umpires and coaches; final authority resting with the plate umpire. Note that state associations may dictate which type of ball is used in state tournaments.

Case 4: Wrapped Bat Handle

The bat is illegal in (a) and legal in (b). Bat handles may not be wrapped with a material or substance that causes the handle to be slippery.

Smooth tape is not allowed because the bat has a greater chance of slipping out of the batter's hands and creating a hazard. If a batter steps into the batter's box with an illegal bat and the pitcher, in position with a live ball, is standing on the pitcher's plate, the batter is immediately out. If the bat handle looks smooth, you may inspect the bat. If the handle is too smooth, the equipment should be prohibited.

Case 5: Incorrectly Set Pitcher's Plate

The distance must be corrected immediately, and all runs from the previous inning count.

Any time a field is discovered to have the pitcher's plate, home plate or bases incorrectly positioned, the situation must be remedied immediately, regardless of any disadvantage experienced by one or both of the teams. Any protest from the disadvantaged team will be rejected because the coaches allowed the game to start on a nonregulation facility, thereby consenting to play even though the field did not meet all rule specifications. Many high school fields are deficient in some part of the field requirements, but when coaches agree to play on such a field or the game is started, all protest rights related to the nonregulation facility are waived.

Case 6: Runner Misses a Base

The runner who did not touch home plate is out on the appeal, and the play on the batter is live, to be appropriately called by the umpire.

A runner may be put out by the defense for missing a base during a live-ball appeal by tagging the runner (even if on another base) or by tagging the missed base and indicating to the umpire what they are appealing. If no member of the defensive team noticed that the runner from third did not touch home plate and the game continued into the next pitch, the run would count and could no longer be appealed. Note that if the catcher enters the bench/dugout area, the ball should be ruled dead and any other runners on base should be awarded one base—the tagging of the runner from third in the dugout should not be allowed, and the defense can still make a dead-ball appeal before the next pitch.

Case 7: A Catch or a Dropped Ball?

In the first two instances, the fielder did not catch the ball. In the third, it is a legal catch if you rule that the ball was dropped as the center fielder attempted to transfer the ball to her throwing hand.

It is up to you to judge whether a fielder had adequate possession of a ball and thus made a catch. Often the judgment to be made is whether the fielder was transferring the ball to the throwing hand when it was dropped or whether the fielder dropped the ball before doing this for another reason. If the ball is dropped while being transferred to the throwing hand, the fielder has caught the ball.

Case 8: Pitcher's Conference

Both conferences are legal and should be allowed. In the first situation, the conference should be charged and recorded as such by the plate umpire. In the second situation, the conference would not be charged because the participants are active, on-field players.

Each team is allowed three charged conferences in a seven-inning game. Each team is granted one charged conference per extra inning while on defense, without any penalty, if a game lasts longer than the standard seven innings.

Case 9: Faked Tag

Yes, the shortstop is guilty of obstruction. If in your judgment the runner could have reached third base if not for the obstruction, the runner is granted third base. Otherwise, you must rule the runner out.

Faking a tag is considered obstruction and is penalized as such. The difficult part of this call is judging what would have happened if the fake tag had not occurred—you must ask yourself whether or not the fake tag actually slowed down the runner. Since the fake-tag obstruction occurred before the runner touched second base, the runner cannot be put out between first and second by rule. If you feel that if the fake tag had not occurred, the runner would have made third, then you should protect her to that base. If she is tagged out prior to third, you would call time and award her third. If you did not feel she would have made third whether or not there was a fake tag, then she is on her own in advancing to third and, if tagged, would remain out.

Case 10: Wrong Uniform Number

Although technically Brown has violated the rule requiring a player's name, shirt number and position to be on the lineup card, there is no penalty because the batting-out-of-order rule only requires that the name be in the proper order. If the number was correct but the player batting was not Brown, the batting-out-of-order penalty would be imposed (see the *NFHS Softball Rules Book* for details).

The listing of both numbers and positions makes for easier record keeping for scorekeepers and umpires, but the name is what counts when it comes to the batting order. Correct the number on your lineup card and move on.

Case 11: An Unlisted Substitute

In both situations, the substitute can be added to the lineup card and is eligible to enter the game as a substitute.

A player who is not listed as an eligible substitute on the lineup card shall not be prohibited from playing. Consider it this way: If the coach made an error and forgot to list someone, it would not be fair to keep a student-athlete out of the game.

Case 12: Uniform Variations
No problem. The uniforms and jackets are legal in all the situations.

The uniforms of all team members should be of the same color and style, and warming jackets are allowed.

Case 13: Uniform Numbers, Logos and Patches
Notify team A's coach of your concern, and verify the size of the numbers with a ruler, if necessary. If the uniform numbers are less than 6 inches high, inform the coach that the team uniforms are not in compliance with the rules but allow the game to continue. You should also notify the state association of the infraction.

Uniforms must always have numbers on the *back* of the shirt or jersey, and they must be at least 6 inches in height. This goes for all players—if a single player has an illegal uniform, you need to notify the coach and the state association.

Case 14: Jewelry and Medical Symbols
The bracelet is legal. Instruct the player and coach that the taping may leave the medical-alert bracelet visible.

Players in the game are prohibited from wearing jewelry such as rings, watches, earrings, bracelets, necklaces (including cloth or string types), barrettes, or other cosmetic or decorative items that are hard. Religious and medical-alert medals are not considered jewelry. A religious medal must be taped and worn under the uniform. A medical-alert medallion or bracelet must be taped and may be visible. All casts, splints and braces must be padded. Prostheses may be worn. As umpire, you have some discretion in this area—any equipment you judge to be dangerous should be prohibited.

Case 15: Substitution During an At Bat
Yes, the substitution can be made. The coach should request a time-out to make the substitution. Upon entering the game, the substitute is charged with one ball and two strikes, the same count that the batter had. If the substitute strikes out, the strikeout is charged against the batter since she had more than half the allotted number of strikes. If the batter had only one or zero strikes on leaving the game, the substitute would be charged with the strikeout.

Case 16: Reentering the Game
No, this is not a legal substitution. Jones may reenter but must remain in the second position in the batting order for the entire game, since that is where she began the game. Jones and Smith are both locked into the second

position in the batting order while in the game; however, they may play various defensive positions. Jones and Smith cannot be in the game at the same time because they must occupy the same slot in the batting order, and two players in the same slot—a starter and her substitute—can never be in the game at the same time. Neither Jones nor Smith may be transferred to any other position in the batting order. All players—starters and substitutes—may reenter only once. *Note:* Starting is considered an entry.

Case 17: DP and the Reentry Rule

Yes, the DP can enter the game defensively for any defensive player. No, the DP plays defense for a player, not a defensive position.

The DP can play defense for any player. If she plays for the FLEX, the FLEX must leave the game (remember, for the FLEX to be considered in the game, she must be playing defense), and the team would be playing with nine. If she plays defense for any other player in the lineup, that player continues to bat (in the same batting position she had been in) and simply does not play a defensive position. The team would still be playing with 10. In the previous case, if the DP wanted to play first base but the coach did not want the FLEX to leave the game, the coach could put the DP on defense for the player playing second base, then make a defensive change—have the first baseman and the second baseman switch positions. This way, the FLEX is still in the game, but she is now playing second base. The DP—who is in the game for the original second baseman—is now playing first base, and the original second baseman is not playing any defensive position but is still batting where she always was.

Case 18: Bleeding Player

The player does not necessarily have to be removed from the game. You must stop play and summon the injured player's coach or trainer to attend to her. If adequate treatment can be administered in a reasonable amount of time, based on umpire judgment, she may resume playing without having to leave the game.

Case 19: Player Throws a Bat

If the act was judged to be intentional, the offender should be ejected from the game. If the batter's fair hit ball is a base hit, the batter must be replaced with a substitute runner. If the act was judged to be unintentional, the umpire should warn the team for a carelessly thrown bat, and if the act is repeated, any subsequent offenders on that team should be restricted to the bench/dugout for the duration of the game.

Bats are obviously dangerous objects, and thus players must take care not to use them in a way that could injure other participants (or you!). If a player throws a bat intentionally, the player should be penalized to discourage similar behavior in the future by other players.

CHAPTER 7

TIMING AND GAME PLAY

Umpiring a softball game is somewhat akin to conducting a symphony, with timing a key factor in overall success. In softball, timing refers to the constant starting and stopping of play as a result of dead ball, delayed dead ball and other rulings that control play.

The two rules covered by the cases in this chapter address pregame procedures, dead-ball situations and more. The rules covered are

- Rule 4: Starting and Ending the Game
- Rule 5: Dead Ball and Suspension of Play

Previous chapters discussed mechanics for getting the game started, ending it properly and managing game situations that require suspension of play. Following are a handful of scenarios that you are likely to run into when you are out on the field; they are designed to illustrate proper rulings for potentially tricky situations. Answers to the cases are included at the end of the chapter so you can verify that you understand the rationale behind the rulings.

Rule 4: Starting and Ending the Game

Do not underestimate the importance of starting and ending games properly. Pregame procedures are extremely important in ensuring that all participants are prepared to play and umpire the game and that the field and all equipment have been thoroughly reviewed and accounted for. Decide how you would make the call, and then check your decision against the answers beginning on page 147 at the end of the chapter.

Starting a Game

Chapter 2 covered pre- and postgame responsibilities of the plate umpire and base umpires, including the pregame conference, the importance of walking the grounds to determine all field anomalies that require special ground rules and other important procedures. Handling pregame steps incorrectly can result in some difficult and embarrassing surprises, so be sure to take the time to get the game started on the right foot!

CASE 1: Ground Rules—Home Run Fence

On arrival, you note that the right-field fence is pretty short at just 180 feet from the plate. During the pregame conference, the opposing coaches agree to a ground rule that provides for a double instead of a home run if the batter hits the ball over the fence. Is this legal?

CASE 2: Muddy Pitcher's Area

Rain begins to fall in the third inning that is heavy enough to dampen the entire field but not to call the game. In the fourth inning, F1 is having a hard time maintaining her footing when pitching. The home team's coach (a) brings in sand to help dry the area around the pitcher's plate or (b) sets up an artificial surface such as a rubber mat for the pitcher to pitch from. Are either of these solutions legal?

Ending a Game

Games often end for reasons other than the completion of seven innings, so you need to be well versed in handling situations that cause a game to end prematurely.

CASE 3: Late-Inning Rainout

During the top of the fifth inning, (a) the score is tied or (b) one of the teams is ahead when rain halts play. You wait a while to see if the skies will clear, but eventually it becomes clear that the game must be ended. What is the official outcome of the game for the scorebooks?

CASE 4: Tiebreaking Procedure

During the pregame conference, both coaches inform you that they mutually agreed to use a tiebreaking procedure if the regulation game ends in a tie. Should you allow this?

A Forfeited Game

As umpire, you should take action to forfeit a game to the nonoffending team if an offending team

- is late in arriving for the game. State associations are authorized to specify the time frame and circumstances for declaring a forfeit due to a late arrival by one of the teams. Be sure you are aware of your state's specific regulations.
- refuses to continue play after the game has started.
- delays more than one minute in beginning play after you call, "Play ball!" or delays in obeying an order to remove a player for violation of the rules.
- persists in tactics designed to delay or shorten the game.
- willfully and persistently violates any of the rules after being warned not to do so.

- is unable to provide 9 players (fast pitch), 10 players (slow pitch) or 11 players (slow pitch if an extra player is used) to start a game. A team shall be allowed to finish a game with 8 players (fast pitch), 9 players (slow pitch) or 10 players (slow pitch if an EP is used), with an out being called in that spot of the batting order.
- on its home field, fails to comply with the umpire's order to put the field in condition for play.

Under official national rules, the score of a forfeited game is recorded as 7 to 0 unless the game is forfeited after the number of innings required for a regulation game have been played and the offending team is behind. The score then remains as occurred in the game. If the offending team is leading, the score is recorded as 7 to 0 in favor of the nonoffending team.

CASE 5: Late Arrival

The visiting team arrives 25 minutes late for a 4:30 game but (a) had called ahead to inform the home team of arriving late or (b) did not call ahead. Does the visiting team automatically forfeit the game?

Rule 5: Dead Ball and Suspension of Play

Many game occurrences create a dead-ball situation, ranging from a hit batter to spectator interference. As umpire, you must frequently stop and restart play throughout the game to enforce rules, awards and penalties. Consider how you'd respond in each situation and check your judgments against the answers beginning on page 148 at the end of the chapter.

Dead Ball

A dead-ball situation means that all play ceases—runners may not advance and the pitcher may not pitch.

CASE 6: Ball Four—Live or Dead Ball?

During a fast-pitch game, a runner is on first when a batter receives a fourth ball. The catcher (a) drops the ball or (b) throws the ball to the pitcher and she drops it. In either case, the runner takes the opportunity to advance to third base.

If the catcher drops the fourth ball, it is still live and legal for a runner to advance.

Is the ball dead after ball four, or is the runner allowed to attempt to advance?

CASE 7: Hit Base Runner or Umpire

A batter hits a ground ball to left field.The left fielder throws the ball to the infield, where it hits an umpire or a base runner. Is the ball dead, or does play continue?

CASE 8: Dead-Ball Territory

On a foul fly ball near dead-ball territory, the left fielder (a) makes the catch with one foot on the line separating live- and dead-ball territory and the other foot in dead-ball territory, (b) makes the catch with one foot in dead-ball territory and then steps with both feet into dead-ball territory or (c) makes the catch with both feet completely in dead-ball territory. In each of these cases, does the catch count?

Delayed Dead Ball

The term *delayed dead ball* refers to situations in which an infraction occurs but play is allowed to continue because it could be advantageous to the offended team. Penalties may or may not be imposed at the end of the action, depending on the outcome of the play. The ball is not declared dead until the natural course of the play is complete or if an obstructed runner is put out prior to reaching the base she would have reached had there been no obstruction. Possible delayed dead-ball situations include illegal pitches, obstruction and interference with the catcher by the plate umpire.

CASE 9: Delayed Dead Ball—Catcher Obstruction

A runner is on third base and a runner is on second base. As the batter attempts to hit the ball, the catcher touches the tip of the batter's bat with her glove or steps on home plate to catch the pitch. What is the correct call, and what happens with the runners?

Suspension of Play

Play may be suspended for several reasons, including umpire or player injury, spectator-created problems, substitutions, or rain or other environmental situations. Any umpire can suspend play, but play is resumed with a "Play ball!" call by the plate umpire.

CASE 10: Batter Time-Out

The pitcher has started to deliver the pitch when the batter requests time and quickly steps out of the batter's box. Do you grant time, and if the pitcher continues her motion and delivers the pitch, does the pitch count?

Answers

Following are the answers to the cases presented in this chapter.

Case 1: Ground Rules—Home Run Fence

No, this is not a legal ground rule, and as umpire, you should not allow it.

Ground rules may not supersede an official rule in the *NFHS Softball Rules Book*. Therefore, a batted ball that clears the fence in fair territory is a home run—end of discussion. This example underscores the importance of having thorough knowledge of all the rules—you never know what unusual local ground rules will be proposed that just might be contrary to an official rule in the *NFHS Softball Rules Book*.

Case 2: Muddy Pitcher's Area

The sand used in (a) is legal, but the rubber mat in (b) is not.

Sand or another approved substance may be used to dry the pitcher's area, but no other platforms may be used. If field conditions are so poor that the safety of the players is in question, you should call the game.

Case 3: Late-Inning Rainout

In both (a) and (b), the game would be called "no game." Because the minimum number of innings for a complete game have not transpired, the game would be called "no game" unless the state association had adopted a game-ending procedure covering such situations (such as a tiebreaking procedure). In (b), it does not matter which team is ahead because fewer than 4 1/2 innings have been completed. Had 4 1/2 innings been completed with the home team leading, the game would be considered regulation and therefore complete. If after 4 1/2 innings the visiting team is leading, the game would not be considered complete because the home team would need to be granted one more opportunity at bat to be fair. Generally, after 30 minutes of rain delay, you may declare the game ended or, by state association adoption, suspended.

Case 4: Tiebreaking Procedure

You should allow this procedure only if your state association has officially adopted it as a game-ending procedure.

Unless your state association has adopted a tiebreaking procedure, this option is not available, even if coaches mutually agree on it during the pregame conference. Make sure you are familiar with any state-specific softball regulations in your area. Your state association may specify procedures and the point in the game at which a procedure will be implemented. This might be after a particular number of innings or a specific time limit.

Case 5: Late Arrival

There is no simple or general rule for declaring when a forfeit should be called as a result of a team arriving late, as the guidelines vary from one state association to another.

In both (a) and (b), you must follow the guidelines set up by your state association to cover circumstances concerning delays. Depending on the state, the decision could go either way. Generally, the spirit of your job as umpire is to get game play under way, but always in a manner that is as fair as possible. If you were to start a game late and it was ultimately called early as a result of darkness *because* the game started late, the team that arrived on time may be unfairly penalized.

Case 6: Ball Four—Live or Dead Ball?

In fast pitch, the ball remains live after ball four is pitched, so R1 is allowed to advance.

Because the ball remains live after a fourth ball, all runners may attempt to advance. The defensive team must maintain control of the ball and be ready to stop runners from advancing in this situation.

Case 7: Hit Base Runner or Umpire

The ball is not dead and play continues. The ball remains live despite hitting an umpire or base runner unless the base runner intentionally caused contact with the ball. Just as you are responsible for knowing the rules, so too are the players and coaches—ignorance of the rules is no excuse!

Case 8: Dead-Ball Territory

The correct ruling is no catch in all situations described, and the ball must be declared dead.

Dead-ball territory is not always well marked, so you will occasionally have to make a determination as to whether a player is in live- or dead-ball territory by quickly moving to the dead-ball line to see if or when the fielder steps out of play. Following are the primary rules for determining whether a fielder is in live- or dead-ball territory:

- If a fielder's feet are touching the line or are in live-ball territory, she is considered in the field of play and may legally field, catch or throw the ball without penalty.
- If a player's entire foot is beyond the line, touching dead-ball territory, when she catches, fields or throws the ball, she has entered dead-ball territory and the ball should be declared dead.

- If a fielder has one foot in play and the other foot in the air, she may legally catch, field or throw the ball until her entire foot contacts the ground in dead-ball territory, at which time the ball becomes dead. The catch is good and results in an out. All runners are awarded one base from the time she stepped into dead-ball territory.

- If a fielder contacts dead-ball territory with any part of the body except the foot, she is considered out of play. If a fielder completely leaves live-ball territory, she must reestablish herself in live-ball territory by having both feet completely in live-ball territory before making a legal catch.

A fielder's contact with dead-ball territory with any part of the body, except the foot, deems her out of play.

Case 9: Delayed Dead Ball—Catcher Obstruction

A delayed dead ball should be signaled as a result of catcher obstruction.

If the batter reaches first base (as a result of a hit, for example) and the runner from third and the runner from second each advance at least one base, the ball remains live and the obstruction is ignored. If the batter and all runners do not advance at least one base, you must give the coach or captain of the team at bat the option of accepting the outcome of the play or the penalty for catcher obstruction. The penalty requires that the batter be awarded first base and the two runners return to third and second bases, respectively, *unless* the runner from third and/or the runner from second were attempting to advance on the pitch. If both runners were attempting to advance on the pitch, you must use your judgment to make sure you do not penalize the batting team for the obstruction (by negating advancement of the runners).

Case 10: Batter Time-Out

Time should not be requested or granted once the pitcher's windup has begun—a legally delivered pitch should count as a strike.

When a batter steps out of the batter's box during a pitch, if the pitcher delivers a legal pitch, it shall be called a strike regardless of the location of the pitch relative to the strike zone. If the pitcher stops or hesitates in her delivery, the umpire shall call, "Time," declare a "no pitch" and start play anew because both the batter and pitcher violated a rule.

CHAPTER 8

PLAY

Once you have taken care of the pregame formalities, it's time to get to the good stuff—actually *playing* the game. Previous chapters covered the umpiring mechanics used to handle game action, and this chapter presents case examples to illustrate the main rules used to make rulings on the action.

This chapter covers the following rules:

- Rule 6: Pitching
- Rule 7: Batting
- Rule 8: Baserunning

Rule 6: Pitching

Whether you are working as the plate umpire or a base umpire, you need to know what constitutes a legal pitch and what actions are illegal. Pitching violations may occur any time the pitcher is in the pitcher's circle until she releases a pitch. Consider how you'd respond in each situation and check your judgments against the answers beginning on page 158 at the end of the chapter.

CASE 1: The Windup
The pitcher waits for a batter to step into the batter's box, then steps forward onto the pitcher's plate with her hands separated. She brings her hands together as she takes a signal from the catcher and immediately begins her windup motion. The batter hits into a double play, and the coach of the batting team promptly argues for an illegal pitch call. Is the pitch legal?

CASE 2: The Windmill Pitch
The pitcher steps onto the pitcher's plate, brings her hands together, and after pausing one second, removes the ball from her glove with her throwing hand and swings her arm backward to approximately shoulder height. The pitcher starts forward into a windmill delivery, releasing the ball the second time it passes her hip. Is this a legal pitch?

CASE 3: Handling an Illegal Pitch

In a fast-pitch game, a runner is on second base when a batter hits an illegal pitch to the outfield for a base hit. However, the runner (a) is thrown out at third base, (b) is thrown out at home or (c) is safe at third base. The first-base umpire gives the delayed dead-ball signal (by extending the left arm horizontally), indicating that the pitch is illegal. The coach of the batting team petitions to you as the plate umpire for a penalty against the pitcher. What is your ruling?

CASE 4: The Pitcher's Plate

In a slow-pitch game, the pitcher has both feet on the pitcher's plate and appears ready to pitch. The pitcher removes one foot by (a) stepping backward off the plate as she delivers the pitch or (b) stepping forward off the 24-inch pitcher's plate toward the batter when pitching the ball. The batter does not swing, but protests that the pitcher has delivered an illegal pitch. What is your ruling?

Rule 7: Batting

Rule 7 covers several aspects of batting, including the batting order, the batter's position and stance relative to the batter's box, batter's time-out, balls and strikes, and more. Following are a few cases based on common umpiring experiences that will help you prepare for actual game play. Consider how you'd respond in each situation and check your judgments against the answers beginning on page 159 at the end of the chapter.

Position and Batting Order

The basic rules governing batting order are as follows: Each player of each team will have one or more turns at bat except a player for whom a DP is being used. A batter must take a position in the batter's box in the order in which that player's name appears on the lineup card. This order must be followed during the entire game except when an entering substitute takes the replaced player's spot in the batting order. A batter is considered to be batting in proper order if that player follows the preceding player in the lineup, even though the preceding batter may have batted out of order. An improper batter is considered to be at bat as soon as one pitch has been thrown while she is in the batter's box. If a batter is discovered to be out of order, time may be requested and the improper batter may be replaced by the proper batter (who must assume the improper batter's ball and strike count), provided the error is recognized before the improper batter is put out or becomes a base runner.

CASE 5: Batting Out of Order

A batter is scheduled to bat, but another batter enters the batter's box instead. With a count of three balls and two strikes on the new batter, the batting infraction is detected (a) by the batter scheduled to bat, (b) by the catcher, (c) by the coach of either team or (d) by you, the umpire. Does the batter scheduled to bat finish the at bat?

CASE 6: Correcting a Batting Order Mistake

The batting order is officially B1, B2, B3, B4. If the third batter (B3) errone-ously completes an at bat in place of the first batter (B1) and the batting infraction is not detected by anyone before a pitch is made to the second batter (B2), is B2 or B4 the next correct batter?

Batting Infractions

As the plate umpire, you need to keep an eye on the batter to watch for several possible batting infractions, including the following, as described in the *NFHS Softball Rules Book*:

- A batter shall not delay the game by failing to take her position in the batter's box within 20 seconds or by stepping out of the box when the pitcher is on the pitcher's plate.
- A batter shall not hit the ball fair or foul while either foot is touching the ground completely outside the lines of the batter's box or while touching the plate. *Note:* A follow-through with the bat may carry one of the batter's feet entirely outside the box so it touches the ground as the ball is leaving the bat. It is customary for the umpire to ignore this if both feet were in legal position at the start of the swing and if it is not considered an attempt to circumvent the spirit of the rule.
- A batter shall not disconcert the pitcher by stepping out of the box on one side of home plate to the box on the other side while the pitcher is in position and ready to pitch.
- A batter shall not permit a pitched ball to touch her.
- A batter shall not interfere with the catcher's fielding or throwing by leaning over home plate, by stepping out of the batter's box, by making any other movement that hinders action at home or the catcher's attempt to make a play on a runner, or by failing to make a reasonable effort to vacate a congested area when there is a throw to home and there is time for the batter to move away.
- If the bat breaks and is hit by the ball or hits a runner or a fielder, no interference is called. If a whole bat is thrown and interferes with a defensive player attempting a play, interference should be called.

CASE 7: Batter Interference?

In play 1, a runner is on second base and a right-handed batter is at the plate. The runner attempts to steal third with the pitch. The catcher's throw to third hits the batter, who is standing in the batter's box but makes no attempt to get out of the way. Is the batter guilty of interference?

In play 2, a runner is on first base and a right-handed batter is at the plate. The runner attempts to steal second with the pitch. The batter takes a powerful swing and misses an outside pitch. Her momentum carries her into the area between the batter's boxes, causing the catcher to bump her while attempting to throw out the stealing runner. Is the batter guilty of interference?

In play 3, a runner is on second base and a right-handed batter is at the plate. The runner attempts to steal third with the pitch. The catcher's throw to third hits the batter, who has left the batter's box and is trying to get out of the way. Is the batter guilty of interference?

CASE 8: Ball Contacts Bat Twice

A batter swings and (a) hits the ball, which strikes home plate and bounces up, hitting the bat while the batter is in the batter's box; (b) after the batter lays down the bat and begins to run toward first, the ball hits the bat in fair territory or (c) while advancing to first, the batter drops the bat to intentionally contact the ball in fair territory. What is your ruling in (a), (b) and (c)?

Rule 8: Baserunning

Rule 8 covers situations that occur on the bases once the batter leaves the batter's box. The mechanics of the plays you are responsible for covering depend on the umpire system you are using and have been covered in detail in previous chapters. The following sections provide cases that illustrate tricky situations you will commonly need to rule on. Consider how you would rule in each situation and check your judgments against the answers beginning on page 160 at the end of the chapter.

Runners and Fielders

A base runner is entitled to a path between the bases that extends 3 feet to either side of the direct line between subsequent bases. The runner may leave this path if no play is being made on her or to avoid a fielder fielding a batted ball. If a tag is attempted on a runner, her base path becomes a straight line—with 3 feet on either side—from her current position to either of the bases she is between.

Between home and first base, base runners must stay within a special running lane (30 feet long and 3 feet wide) or be liable for interference with the fielder taking the throw at first base.

CASE 9: Runner Hit by Fielder's Throw

With a runner on third base, a batter hits a fair ground ball to the first baseman, who fields the ball just behind first base. The first baseman throws to the catcher, attempting to retire the runner at the plate. The batter (a) moves inside the base path and blocks the throw to home with her body or (b) is hit by the ball while running in fair territory just inside the baseline toward first base. The runner scores and the batter continues to first base. In both (a) and (b), does the run count? Is the batter out or safe?

A run does not count when a runner interferes with a thrown ball.

CASE 10: Runner Interference

With two outs and no runners on base, a batter has a count of three balls and two strikes. On the next pitch, the batter swings and misses. The ball bounces off the catcher's shin guard and lands in front of home plate. The catcher quickly moves out in front of the plate to field the ball, and the batter runs into her and knocks her down, allowing the batter to run safely to first base. The batter has a right to run to first base because the catcher dropped the third strike, but should the batter be allowed to run to first base safely?

CASE 11: Fielder Obstruction

With a runner on second and a runner on first, a batter hits the ball toward the second baseman. While the second baseman is attempting to field the ball, the third baseman takes a step forward, entering the runner from seconds's path as the runner from second is attempting to advance to third on the hit. What is the correct call?

CASE 12: Detached Equipment

A runner is on second base and a runner is on first when a batter hits a ground ball to the shortstop. The shortstop fields the ball, steps on second to force out the runner from first and then throws wildly to the first baseman. The first baseman tosses her glove into the air in an attempt to knock down the throw. The glove hits the ball and causes it to bounce into the dugout. Is the runner from first out? Are there any further rulings on the play?

The Infield-Fly Rule

The infield-fly rule is designed to prevent the defensive team from gaining an unfair advantage when a ball is hit in the air in the infield when there are fewer than two outs and runners on first and second or the bases are loaded. The rule is designed to prevent a fielder from simply letting the ball drop and scooping it up on the first bounce, thereby creating one heck of an opportunity to get a double or even a triple play because the runners cannot leave their bases until the ball is caught!

Instead of allowing such a situation, any time there are fewer than two outs and runners (a) on first and second base or (b) on first, second and third base, if the batter hits a fair fly ball (not including a line drive or an attempted bunt) that can be caught by an infielder with ordinary effort, you must invoke the infield fly rule by calling, "Infield fly! The batter is out!" loud enough for everyone to hear. This call provides important information to fielders and runners. The call signals that

- the batter-runner is out immediately, whether or not the ball is caught,
- the base runners are no longer forced to leave their bases and
- any defensive player in the infield at the time of the pitch shall be considered an infielder for purposes of this rule.

After the call, the ball is live, meaning that runners may tag up and attempt to advance as soon as the batted ball is touched by a fielder. If a declared infield fly becomes foul, it is treated as a foul ball, not an infield fly. When an infield fly is hit close to the line, the umpire should say, "Infield fly! The batter is out if fair!"

The Bases

You must always watch carefully to make sure each runner touches the base they are passing and be ready to handle any appeal that is raised. As there is often more than one runner on the bases, and you need to be watching the fielders and know where the ball is as well, this is not as easy as it sounds.

If you see a runner miss a base, make a mental note of which runner missed which base and keep tracking the action. You are likely to be called on to share this information through the appeal process. Note that you should not volunteer this information—it is up to the defensive team to ask for a ruling.

CASE 13: Missed Base

With a runner on first, a batter singles. The runner rounds second and continues on to third base, but you notice that the runner clearly fails to touch second. What do you do?

CASE 14: Retouching the Base

A runner is on first when a batter hits a deep fly ball to right field. The runner goes halfway to second base before the right fielder makes a great diving catch. The right fielder then throws wildly to the first base-man, and the ball rolls quickly into the stands before the runner returns to first base. The runner goes to third on the award without retouching first base. When the plate umpire throws a new ball to the pitcher, the first baseman makes a dead-ball appeal that the runner did not retouch first base. Is the runner out or safe?

CASE 15: Two Runners on One Base

With a runner on third, a runner on second and a runner on first, the runner from first legally steals second, but the runner from second does not advance, leaving both runners on second base. The pitcher receives the ball in the pitcher's circle from the catcher and makes no play on any runner. May both runners remain at second? If not, what is the correct ruling?

CASE 16: Runner Passes Another Runner

With a runner on first, a batter hits a ground ball to the right fielder. The right fielder fields the ball and throws to third after the runner has rounded second, driving the runner back to second. The batter is moving quickly and rounds second, passing the runner. The third baseman throws wildly to the second baseman at second base and the ball goes into right center field. The runner advances to third and the batter retreats back to second. Are the runner and batter safe at third and second, respectively?

Tagging Up on a Fly Ball

If a fly ball is hit that does not fall under the infield-fly rule and there is a runner on base, that runner may legally advance as soon as the ball is touched, regardless of whether the catch is made

Runners must run the bases in the same order as they bat.

in fair or foul territory. As an umpire, your job is to watch the runner and the fielder to make sure the runner does not leave the base before the ball is first touched.

CASE 17: Runner Leaves the Base Too Early

Runners are on third, second and first base, with no outs when a batter hits a long fly ball to the right fielder. The runner from second leaves second base before the right fielder catches the ball and the runner from third leaves third after the catch and advances to home. The right fielder throws home, but the runner scores before the catcher can field the throw. The catcher throws the ball to the second baseman, who tags out the runner from first at second. The second baseman returns the ball to the pitcher, who is standing off the pitcher's plate. The pitcher asks for time and makes a dead-ball appeal on the runner from second for leaving second base too soon. What is the ruling on the runner from second?

Answers

Following are the answers to the cases presented in this chapter.

Case 1: The Windup

The pitch is legal and the coach of the batting team is mistaken.

A one-second pause is not required after the pitcher's hands are brought together before beginning the windup. The rule states that the hands shall be brought together for at least one second before releasing the ball. This one second may transpire during the windup, prior to delivery. In fast-pitch softball, if the pitch had been illegal (the pitcher did not have both hands on the ball for at least one second), the coach of the team at bat should be given the option of the outcome of the play (because you must call a delayed dead ball on an illegal pitch) or the award. If the award is taken, all runners advance one base and a ball is called on the batter. In slow pitch, the illegal pitch is ignored and the play outcome stands.

Case 2: The Windmill Pitch

Yes, this is a perfectly legal pitch. The starting point of the pitching motion is defined as where the pitcher's arm starts forward; in this case, behind her body at shoulder height. Even though the ball passed her hip twice, the pitcher's arm did not make two complete revolutions. The official rule states that a pitcher's arm may not make two full revolutions. In the example described in this case, the pitcher's arm did not make two revolutions.

Case 3: Handling an Illegal Pitch

For fast pitch, in the event of (a), (b) and (c), you should give the coach of the team at bat the option of accepting the outcome of the play or taking the penalty for an illegal pitch.

The penalty for an illegal pitch is that all runners advance one base and a ball is added to the pitch count on the batter.

Case 4: The Pitcher's Plate
For slow pitch, (a) is illegal because the pitcher stepped backward. It is not necessary for the pitcher to take a step at all, but if a step is taken, it *must* be forward and simultaneous with the release of the ball. In (b), the pitch is entirely legal because the non-pivot foot does not need to be within the 24-inch width of the pitcher's plate.

Case 5: Batting Out of Order
The batter does not finish the at bat. In (a), (b) and (c), the situation is correctable as long as the improper batter is still at bat. Once the mistake is identified, another batter should take the place of the first batter at the plate with whatever pitch count exists—in this case, a count of three balls and two strikes. Before a pitch, you may ask the improper batter if she should be at bat. After the first pitch is made, you should remain silent. In (d), where you are the one who identifies the batting order problem, you should remain silent.

Case 6: Correcting a Batting Order Mistake
B4 is the next batter and should replace B2 at the plate because her name follows that of B3 on the lineup card. Neither B1 nor B2 may legally bat until their time comes again as listed. If an improper batter becomes a runner or is put out and (a) a legal or illegal pitch is delivered to the succeeding batter, (b) an intentional base on balls (slow pitch) has occurred or (c) all infielders have left the diamond because a half inning has ended before an appeal is made, then the improper batter becomes the proper batter and the results of her time at bat become legal. The next batter should be the batter whose name follows that of the now legalized improper batter. The instant an improper batter's actions are legalized, the batting order picks up with the name following that of the legalized improper batter.

Case 7: Batter Interference?
In play 1, the batter is not guilty of interference, but in plays 2 and 3, the batters have committed interference.

In play 1, the batter's box is not a sanctuary, but in order for a batter to be called out for interference while still in the batter's box, she must do something intentional to interfere. The batter's box belongs to the batter. Everywhere else on the field belongs to the catcher.

In play 2, the batter can swing however she chooses; she can follow through with the swing, and she can allow her momentum to take her anywhere. But when the pitch is over, she cannot interfere. If any of these acts interferes with the catcher's attempt to make a play on a runner, then it is interference and the batter is out.

In play 3, the batter is not immune from interference while in the batter's box; however, to be ruled out for interference while in the batter's box, the batter must, in the umpire's judgment, intentionally interfere. The batter is liable for interference when out of the batter's box whether or not the act is intentional.

Case 8: Ball Contacts Bat Twice

In (a), it is a foul ball; in (b), the ball remains live; and in (c), the batter is out and the ball is dead.

In (a), the batter is still in the batter box, the bat is still in the batter's hands and the batter did nothing intentional when the ball strikes the bat a second time, and thus it must be called a foul ball. In (b), as long as you judge the second bat-ball contact to be accidental (the ball traveled into the bat and the batter has no control over the ball), there is no call to be made—the ball remains live. In (c), the batter has clearly attempted to gain an unfair advantage and must be penalized by being put out.

Case 9: Runner Hit by Fielder's Throw

In (a), the runner's run does not count and the batter is out for interference. In (b), the run counts and the batter safely takes first base.

In (a), the violation is not 3-foot-lane interference; it is runner interference with a thrown ball. B2 intentionally interfered with the first baseman's throw to the catcher, which is illegal. The ball is dead, the runner is sent back to third base and the batter is out for interference. In (b), the batter was legally running the bases and did nothing intentional to interfere with the throw. The ball is live, the runner scores and the batter is safe at first. This is not 3-foot-lane interference because it did not involve a fielder taking the throw at first base. It is also not runner interference because the batter was not yet out, did nothing intentional and was legally running the bases. If this were considered interference, fielders would simply throw and hit the runners.

Case 10: Runner Interference

No, the batter has caused runner interference by running into the catcher intentionally. Because the catcher had already moved out in front of the plate, the batter had a clear path to first base. You would immediately make a dead-ball call and rule the batter-runner out for interference (you need to verbalize the interference call so everyone understands why the batter is out). In addition, if there are any runners on base, they must return to the last base legally touched at the time of the interference.

Case 11: Fielder Obstruction

The correct call is obstruction on the part of the third baseman. Since the third baseman is not fielding a batted ball, she cannot, in any fashion, block or impede the progress of a runner running the bases. Give the delayed dead-ball signal and mentally decide how far the runner from second could have gotten had there been no obstruction. By rule, the runner from second cannot be put out between second and third (the bases she was obstructed between), so you should protect her at least to third base. If in your judgment she could have reached home had there been no obstruction, then you should protect her to the plate. If you judge that she could not have made home, then she advances beyond third at her own risk, and if put out after reaching third, she remains out.

Case 12: Detached Equipment

The runner from first is out on the force play. An additional ruling must be made, however, because the first baseman violated the detached equipment rule by throwing her glove in the air and contacting the ball. Both the runner from second and the batter are awarded two bases from where they were positioned when the violation occurred.

The detached equipment rule exists to prevent players from using equipment in ways other than those it was designed for. As umpire, you must give a delayed dead-ball signal any time you see an infraction of this nature during live-ball play. Remember, the glove must actually contact the ball. Simply throwing the glove (and missing the ball) is not a violation.

In this case, the first award is two bases (from the last base touched at the time of the throw) to the runner being played on, but the ball remains live and she can advance further at her own risk. Then, when the ball enters the dugout, the ball must be ruled dead, and all runners are awarded two bases from the last base touched at the time of the throw. The batter had not reached first base at the time of the throw, so she would be awarded second base. The runner from second was somewhere between second and third or third and home and in either case would be awarded home.

Case 13: Missed Base

If there is no appeal before the pitcher throws the next pitch, you can forget all about it. But if the defensive team appeals, asking for a ruling, you must indicate what you saw—that the runner missed the base.

If appealed properly by the defensive team, you must call the runner out for failing to touch second base. An appeal can be made until a subsequent pitch has been delivered (whether a legal or illegal pitch). If the ball becomes dead on the same play that a runner misses a base, the appeal can still be made. An appeal can even be made after the umpire has called, "Play ball!" after a dead-ball period, as long as a pitch has not been delivered.

Case 14: Retouching the Base

The runner is called out on the appeal for not retouching first base. Because the runner was between second and first when the ball went out of play, she could have legally retouched first before taking her award. The umpire should give her the opportunity to do so prior to awarding bases, but if she does not do so in a timely manner, the umpire must simply award the bases—second and third, two bases from the last base touched at the time of the throw.

The umpire would not allow a dead-ball appeal until the runner has completed her baserunning responsibilities. After the umpire puts a new ball in play, and before a pitch to another batter, the defense can make a dead-ball appeal. The runner left first base before the fly ball was first touched and did not return and retouch the base, so she is called out on the appeal.

Case 15: Two Runners on One Base

No, two runners can never remain on a single base. After allowing a reasonable amount of time for a play to be made, you must declare a ball dead and call the runner from first out, even if no tag is made.

This rule is simple—two runners may not occupy the same base simultaneously. In this example, the runner from first can be tagged out if both runners are standing on second base. The runner who first legally occupied the base—in this case, the runner from second—shall be entitled to it unless forced to advance.

In another example, the runner from second begins a play on second base, and the runner from first is on first. The batter hits a ground ball and runs to first. The runner from first runs to second. The runner from second is forced to run to third but does not. In this case, because the runner from second should have run to third, the runner from second is the runner who can be put out with a tag if both the runner from second and the runner from first are standing on second base.

Case 16: Runner Passes Another Runner

No, the batter is out as soon as she passes the runner on the base paths, but the ball remains live. The runner's advance to third is legal.

Base runners must run the bases in the same order as they bat. If one runner passes another, the runner doing the passing is called out and the ball remains live.

Case 17: Runner Leaves the Base Too Early

You must declare the runner from second out for leaving second base before the right fielder touched the ball. However, the runner from third's run counts because she crossed home plate before the third out, which was not a force-out.

The play in this example is a "timing" play. The runner from third's run counts because it occurred before the third out of the inning was made and it was not a force-out. If a runner reaches home an instant before the last out (which is not a force-out) is made, then the run is scored. If a runner reaches home an instant after the last out is made (which, again, is not a force-out), no run would be scored. If the third out is made by a force-out, it does not matter when the run was scored; it does not count.

CHAPTER 9

KEEPING IT FAIR

In addition to the challenge of making good calls and maintaining control of the game, an umpire also needs to understand the nuances of official scoring. Should a hit be ruled a sacrifice fly or simply an out? Was that fantastic hit actually a home run or just a four-base award? What if a runner on first steals second base just as the pitcher delivers an illegal pitch? Does the runner get credited with a steal?

Rule 9, Scoring and Record Keeping, covers some highly specific instances when the offensive team sends a runner across the plate and also touches on how plays should be scored officially so the next day's newspaper gets things right. Rule 10, Umpiring, provides extra guidance for umpires and details the duties, responsibilities, procedures and uniform for umpires.

The cases in this chapter provide insight into a few situations you are likely to encounter on the field, but as always, be sure to review the *NFHS Softball Rules Book* and the complete *NFHS Softball Case Book* to make sure you know your stuff before you get on the field and under the microscope!

Rule 9: Scoring and Record Keeping

Although the official rules state that "the team whose runners score the greatest total number of runs for the entire regulation game wins," you can probably guess that managing the scoring aspect of the game gets a little more complicated than the rules sound!

You can reasonably expect that the official scorekeeper (if there is one for the game) will know the game of softball quite well, but you, as the umpire, are still the official arbiter of how plays get recorded in the books. As part of calling the game, you often need to make some fine distinctions in how plays occur to get the actual scoring right. However, scoring is not your job, and you should never give an opinion on whether a play is a hit or an error or make any other judgment about scoring. Consider how you'd respond in each situation and check your judgments against the answers beginning on page 166.

Managing runs effectively requires you to be alert from the pitch to the score.

Scoring

One aspect of umpiring you must know backward and forward is determining when runs count and when they do not. This is likely to be the most controversial aspect of a game, so you need to know the rules and be ready to "sell" the call with all you've got.

CASE 1: Walking in a Run

With two outs and three runners on base, a batter receives ball four. The runner from first touches second but then wanders off the bag and is tagged for the third out before the runner from third reaches home plate to score. Does the runner from third's run count?

CASE 2: Missed Base—Run Scores

With one out and a runner on third base, a runner on second and runner on first, a batter hits safely to right field. The runner from third scores; the runner from second does not touch third base but continues on to score; the right fielder throws out the runner from first with a great throw to third base. At the end of playing action, the defensive team makes a dead-ball appeal that the runner from second missed third on her way home. You agree and declare the runner from second out. How many runs score?

Official Scoring for Batting, Running and Fielding

Not all teams keep detailed statistics, but many do, so you will need to be clear on how things officially occur in addition to making the correct calls.

CASE 3: Scoring the Run

With a runner on third base, a runner on second and runner on first, a batter hits a long fly ball to center field that is caught by the center fielder. The runner from third advances to the plate. The center fielder throws to second base (a) in time to retire the runner from first attempting to advance or (b) not in time to get the runner from first. How is the run scored, and how are all advances recorded?

CASE 4: Attempted Steal

In a fast-pitch game, a runner attempts to steal second base when you call the pitcher for an illegal pitch. The runner reaches second after the pitch with no throw from the catcher. Does the runner get credited with a steal?

CASE 5: Missed Fly Ball

A batter hits a pop-up behind second base that could easily be caught by either the second baseman or the shortstop, but neither fielder catches the ball. What is the official scoring for the play?

Rule 10: Umpiring

Rule 10 gives umpires some guidance and all-encompassing rules to cover miscellaneous situations and unpredictable game events that can surprise even the most experienced official. However, things can occur that are not covered by any rule. Rule 10 gives the plate umpire the authority to make final decisions on points not covered by the rules. Consider how you would respond in each situation and check your judgments against the answers begining on page 167 at the end of the chapter.

CASE 6: Proper Catcher's Equipment

You arrive at the field and observe the catcher warming up the pitcher without the required equipment (a) within or (b) outside the confines of the field. In both (a) and (b), what do you do?

CASE 7: A Possible Rainout

After several innings have been played, it starts to rain, and you decide to suspend play. If rain that is hard enough to prevent play continues for 30 minutes, must the game be called?

CASE 8: Umpire Mistake—Steal on a Walk

In a fast-pitch game, with a runner on first and a three-ball, two-strike count on a batter, the runner attempts to steal second on the next pitch, which turns out to be ball four. The base umpire, the runner and the second baseman do not realize it was ball four, and the runner is called out on the play. The runner heads for the bench and is tagged out during the confusion. As the plate umpire, how do you address the situation?

CASE 9: Umpire Mistake—Infield Fly

With a runner on third and no outs, the batter hits a high fly in the infield above the second-base player's head. A base umpire erroneously calls, "Infield fly, the batter is out!" The second baseman subsequently drops the ball. The runner from third scores, and the batter ends up on second base. Does the play stand, or is the batter out? Does the run count?

The plate umpire has the authority to make final play decisions not covered by the rules.

CASE 10: Checked Swing With a Runner on Base

With a count of three balls and two strikes on a batter and a runner on first base, the batter takes what appears to be a half swing. You call ball four, and the runner, on hearing ball four, trots to second base. The catcher throws the ball to the second baseman, who tags the runner before she reaches the base. The catcher then asks the plate umpire to check with the base umpire to see whether the batter did, in fact, attempt to hit the pitch. The base umpire indicates that the batter did swing at the ball, thereby changing the walk to a strikeout. What do you do with the runner?

Answers

Following are the answers to the cases presented in this chapter.

Case 1: Walking in a Run

Yes, the run counts. The runner from third was entitled to home plate as soon as ball four was declared, and thus the run counts no matter what the relative timing is between the runner from first getting tagged out and the runner from third crossing the plate. The run counts, and the inning is over.

Case 2: Missed Base—Run Scores

No runs score. Because the putout of the runner from second at third base was a force-out, no runs can score (no runs can ever score on a play where the third out of an inning is made by way of a force play or if the batter does not reach first base). The batter becoming a batter-runner forced the runner from second to advance to third. Even though the runner from first—a runner behind the runner from second—was eventually put out, at the time the runner from second failed to touch third, she was forced to it. When appealed, it remains a force-out.

Case 3: Scoring the Run

In both (a) and (b), the runner from third scores by virtue of a sacrifice fly. The runner from second advances to third on a fielder's choice. In (b), the runner from first advances on a fielder's choice.

Any time a run scores as a result of a fly ball that is caught, the run is scored as a sacrifice fly (of course, there must be fewer than two outs for this to occur; if there were two outs, the run would not count because the batter never legally reached first base). The base advances are considered fielder's choices in this example because the center fielder could have made a play on either the runner from second or the runner from from first.

Case 4: Attempted Steal

In fast pitch, the runner is entitled to a stolen base only if, in the scorekeeper's judgment, the runner would have reached second base safely if the illegal pitch had not occurred.

As soon as the illegal pitch occurred, you needed to give a delayed dead-ball signal. The runner's efforts should not be discounted if the runner would have stolen second base legitimately had the illegal pitch not occurred. This is the official scorekeeper's call, but you should be aware of the reasoning behind the ruling. Note also that a ball would be called on the batter as a result of the illegal pitch.

Case 5: Missed Fly Ball

Since the ball should have been caught, it must be an error. Since either the second baseman or the shortstop could have caught the ball, it is scored as a team error and not a hit.

A player is charged with an error for each misplay that prolongs the time at bat of the batter or the time a player continues to be a runner, or for any misplay that permits the runner to advance one or more bases.

Case 6: Proper Catcher's Equipment

Your jurisdiction as umpire begins as soon as you enter the confines of the field. Therefore, in case (a), you should tell the catcher she must wear the required protective equipment. In case (b), you should inform the catcher's coach that the catcher is not wearing the required equipment.

Always keep in mind that part of your job is to help minimize risk to the players, so if there is action you can take to reduce risk, do so.

Case 7: A Possible Rainout

You may call the game when you believe that the field conditions make it impossible to continue play. It is customary to wait 30 minutes before making such an announcement to allow a chance for conditions to improve. Take into consideration that one or both teams may have traveled a great distance to play the game—rescheduling can be difficult and expensive, and more than anything, the players are there to play!

However, if there is still doubt as to whether or not the game may be resumed after 30 minutes, hold your postponement announcement for a reasonable amount of time until you are certain that no further play will be possible. Note that state associations are allowed to create policies involving game-ending procedures, and you should be aware of those in your area. The length of time to wait for a late-arriving team and the length of time to stay in a rain delay are both examples of policies that may vary from state to state.

Case 8: Umpire Mistake—Steal on a Walk

If this occurs in a fast-pitch game, you should clarify for all parties that the batter has walked as a result of a fourth ball and should return the runner to second base.

This ruling falls into both the "commonsense" and "spirit of the game" categories. It is also supported by the rule that says umpires can rectify any situation in which an umpire's decision that was reversed has placed either team in jeopardy. The runner was put out as a result of the umpire's mistaken decision. Umpiring mistakes do happen, but players should never be penalized for them. If this occurs, do your best to fix the situation in as fair a manner as possible. In such cases, it is always wise to consult with the other umpires on your crew.

Case 9: Umpire Mistake—Infield Fly

In this case, the play would stand despite the obvious and embarrassing umpiring error. Although this is clearly a mistake by the base umpire, both teams have a responsibility to know when conditions exist for an infield fly. The batter-runner should attempt to reach base safely despite the umpire's error. The umpire blew the call—but players have *some* responsibility for knowing the rules.

Case 10: Checked Swing With a Runner on Base

You must declare the batter out and return the runner safely to first base. As the plate umpire, you can rectify any situation in which an umpire's decision that was ultimately reversed placed either team at a disadvantage. Always keep the spirit of fair play in mind, and make any corrections in a way that is as fair as possible to both teams.

APPENDIX

NFHS Officiating Softball Signals

A. Do Not Pitch

B. Play Ball

C. Time-Out, Foul Ball or Dead Ball

D. Delayed Dead Ball

E. Strikeout

F. Infield Fly

G. Safe

H. Fair Ball

I. Foul Tip

J. Count

GLOSSARY

appeal play—A play in which a coach appeals a play, believing that the other team broke the rules in some way. Examples include batting out of order, requesting assistance on a batter's half swing, a runner missing a base and a runner leaving a base too soon on a tag-up play.

baseline—The direct line between bases. A runner is out if she runs more than 3 feet out of the baseline to avoid being tagged or to hinder a fielder, unless the runner is trying to avoid interfering with the fielder as the fielder is attempting to field a batted ball. The base runner establishes her own baseline directly between her position and the base she is advancing to.

base umpire—An umpire assigned to a base—first, second or third.

checked swing—Occurs when a batter starts to swing and then stops. The final decision is based on whether the batter struck at the ball.

conference—A conference is charged when a coach meets with a player or players on her team. On defense, a team cannot be granted more than three conferences per seven-inning game. On offense, a team cannot have more than one charged conference per inning.

dead ball—In numerous situations, the ball becomes dead and a play is over. See Rule 5 in the *NFHS Softball Rules Book*.

delayed dead ball—A play in which the ball becomes dead only after the umpire calls, "Time!"

Designated Player (DP/FLEX) Rule—Replaced Designated Hitter (DH) rule for 2004 season. Under this rule, the role of an offensive player is never terminated. DP refers to the player who is batting for the defensive "FLEX" player. Allows both the DH and the FLEX player to play defense simultaneously.

double first base—Two bases that are side by side at first. The white base is in fair territory and is used by the fielder; a colored base is in foul territory and is used by the batter-runner only on the initial play at first base. The double first base is designed to reduce the chance of collision at first base.

fair ball—A batted ball that settles in fair ground between home and third base or between home and first base, or is on or over fair ground when bounding to the outfield past first or third base.

foul ball—A batted ball that settles in foul ground between home and third base or between home and first base, or that bounds past first or third base on or over foul territory and first touches ground in foul territory beyond first or third base.

ground rules—Rules specific to a particular playing field, created to handle field characteristics that do not conform to official NFHS field specifications. Ground rules should be discussed in the pregame conference.

illegal pitch—With any illegal pitch, the ball becomes dead at the end of playing action. A ball is called on the batter, and base runners are awarded one base without liability of being put out. Or, if the batter makes contact with the ball, the coach of the team at bat shall have the option of the result of the play or the penalty for an illegal pitch. Examples of illegal pitches include use of a "crow hop" or "leap."

illegally batted ball—A ball hit while breaking a rule, such as batting with a foot touching the ground completely outside the lines of the batter's box or touching home plate. The ball is dead and the batter is out.

infield fly—A fair fly ball (not a line drive or an attempted bunt) that an infielder can catch with ordinary effort with less than two outs with runners on first and second or with the bases loaded. The batter is automatically out.

interference—Can occur in a number of situations when a batter or base runner interferes with the fielding of, or throwing of, the ball.

National Operating Committee on Standards for Athletic Equipment (NOCSAE)—Governing body for the approval of athletic equipment. All batting and catcher's helmets must display the NOCSAE logo.

obstruction—Obstruction occurs in a number of instances when a fielder hinders the progress of a base runner. Obstruction can be intentional, such as a fake tag, or unintentional, such as when the defensive player is illegally in the path of the runner. The umpire has the authority to determine what base to award to the runner.

out—A batter makes an out in numerous ways, including hitting a fair or foul ball caught by a fielder, striking out, bunting foul on the third strike, hitting a ball that is ruled an infield fly and being thrown out at first on a ground ball.

plate umpire—The umpire behind the plate, also known as the umpire-in-chief.

pregame conference—Meeting held prior to start of the game with all officials, both coaches and the captains of each team to review lineups, discuss ground rules and answer any questions.

strike—A strike is recorded in various situations, including a swing and miss by a batter, a called strike taken by a batter, a pitch hit foul and a pitch bunted foul.

strike zone— Fast pitch (FP): The strike zone is the space over home plate which is between the batter's forward armpit and the top of the knees when the batter assumes a natural batting stance. Slow pitch (SP): The strike zone is the space over home plate which is between the batter's highest shoulder and the knees when the batter assumes a natural batting stance.

suspended game—A called game to be completed at a later date.

three-foot lane—The lane drawn over the last half of the distance to first base. The batter-runner must stay inside this lane while the ball is being fielded or thrown to first base, unless in doing so she will interfere with the fielding or throwing of the ball.

time-out (immediate dead ball)—The ball becomes dead immediately in a number of situations, including when a pitch touches the batter or her clothing (even if the batter swings at it), when a foul ball is not caught, when an umpire calls interference, when a fair batted ball touches a runner or umpire before touching any fielder and before passing any fielder other than the pitcher, and when a spectator touches a ball.

INDEX

The italicized *f* following page numbers refers to figures.

ABOUT THE AUTHOR

Officiating Softball was written by the American Sport Education Program (ASEP) in cooperation with the National Federation of State High School Associations (NFHS). Based in Indianapolis, the NFHS is the rules authority for high school sports in the United States. Hundreds of thousands of officials nationwide and throughout the world rely on the NFHS for officiating guidance. ASEP is a division of Human Kinetics, based in Champaign, Illinois, and has been a world leader in providing educational courses and resources to professional and volunteer coaches, officials, parents and sport administrators for more than 20 years. ASEP and the NFHS have teamed up to offer courses for high school officials through the NFHS Officials Education Program.

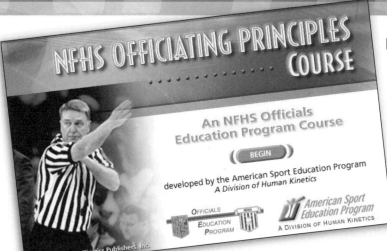